AF673717

Spirituality within You!

Spirituality within You!

MANISHA KOUSHIK

PRABHAT
PRAKASHAN

No part of this publication can be reproduced, stored in a retrieval system or transmitted in any form or by any means, electronic, mechanical, photocopying, recording or otherwise, without prior permission of the author. Rights of this book are reserved with the author.

Published by
PRABHAT PRAKASHAN PVT. LTD.
4/19 Asaf Ali Road,
New Delhi-110 002 (INDIA)
e-mail: prabhatbooks@gmail.com

ISBN 978-93-5521-893-3
SPIRITUALITY WITHIN YOU!
by Manisha Koushik

© Reserved

Edition
First, 2023

Price
₹ 300 (Rupees Three Hundred Only)

Printed at
Japan Art, Delhi

Preface

What is Spirituality?

Spirituality is a fascinating and deep concept that has been explored and practiced for centuries by people worldwide. Spirituality is concerned with the search for greater meaning, purpose and connection in life. It involves exploring the inner self and connecting with a higher power or consciousness that transcends individual identity and ego.

The primary purpose of spirituality is to help individuals connect with their inner self and tap into a deeper sense of purpose and meaning in life. This is often achieved through various practices such as meditation, prayer, introspection and self-reflection, which allow individuals to transcend their limited perceptions and access a higher level of consciousness.

Throughout the following chapters, we will explore the various aspects of spirituality in more detail. We will discuss its history, philosophy and practical applications, and provide insights into how spirituality can be used to cultivate greater awareness, compassion and wisdom in everyday life.

Imagine being in a room with 30 people of different beliefs and backgrounds. Some are devoutly religious, while others have walked away from religion or are still searching for the right one. But here is the kicker—regardless of their beliefs, every single person in that room has spirituality within them. Some may know and connect to it often and some may be completely new to the concept.

Spirituality is not just some abstract concept or New Age buzzword. It is actually the way in which we live our lives. The term 'spirituality' is derived from the Latin word 'spiritus', meaning breath or life. And since life is the most precious gift we have, it makes sense that spirituality is all about how we live that gift.

One important distinction to note is that spirituality is not the same as religion. While religion is often tied to specific beliefs, practices and traditions associated with a particular faith or community, spirituality is a more personal and individualised journey. It is not necessarily tied to any specific religious doctrine or dogma and can be practiced by people of all faiths or no faith at all.

Healthy spirituality is all about connection, mindfulness and celebrating life. But unhealthy spirituality is the opposite—it is characterised by disconnection, lack of awareness, and a negative attitude towards life.

In summary, spirituality offers a powerful way of exploring the deeper aspects of the human experience and finding greater meaning and purpose in life. Through this journey, we can connect with our inner self and tap into a higher level of consciousness, leading to a more fulfilling and meaningful life. So, if you are looking to improve your spiritual well-being, start by taking a closer look at your way of life.

❑

Acknowledgements

Writing this spiritual book has been an extraordinary voyage. I am deeply grateful for the unwavering support and love bestowed upon me by my cherished family, friends and well-wishers. Their encouragement and active involvement throughout this transformative journey have made it an enriching and memorable experience.

I am filled with a profound appreciation for the boundless blessings and unwavering grace of Maa Durga, who has guided me through this intense expedition. Her divine presence has been a constant source of strength, enabling me to triumph over every obstacle with resilience and unwavering determination.

My heartfelt thanks to my father, mentor and guide, Astrologer Dr Prem Kumar Sharma, whose continuous support, guidance and inspiration have been invaluable. His unwavering belief in my abilities has instilled the confidence to confront challenges and strive for excellence.

My better half, Vinay, has been an inexhaustible source of encouragement, propelling me to reach new heights and accomplish more. His enduring support, love, patience and understanding have been the solid foundation of my achievements, and I am immensely grateful for his presence in my life.

Lastly, I extend special gratitude to my son, Nishchay, whose untiring faith in me and unwavering cooperation have driven this endeavour. His encouragement and steadfast support have given me the strength and conviction to pursue my dreams confidently.

In conclusion, the culmination of this spiritual book is a testament to the love, support and guidance of all those who have played a significant role in my journey. Thank you for your persistent presence and active participation in this extraordinary expedition.

❑

Contents

Exploring Spirituality – A Beginner's Guide

Acknowledge and respect the efforts of those who have come before us

Throughout history, individuals have sought to understand their place in the universe and the nature of their existence. The pursuit of spirituality has been a central part of this endeavour, with many dedicating their lives to exploring the mysteries of the divine. From the ancient wisdom of indigenous cultures to the teachings of modern-day spiritual leaders, the quest for spiritual enlightenment has taken many forms.

It is crucial to acknowledge and honour the contributions of those who have come before us in this journey. Their insights and wisdom, regardless of their religious or cultural background, can provide valuable guidance and inspiration for our own spiritual growth. By embracing the experiences and teachings of others, we can learn from their successes and mistakes and gain a deeper understanding of the spiritual path.

At the same time, it is important to recognise that spirituality is a deeply personal and individual journey. While we can draw inspiration and guidance from the experiences of others, ultimately, each person must chart their own course and find their own way. By combining the insights of the past with our own unique perspective and experiences, we can create a spiritual practice that is authentic and meaningful to us.

You are your journey's owner, remember this!

Your spiritual journey is an intimate and personal experience that is shaped by your beliefs, experiences and perceptions. It is a journey that requires introspection, self-reflection, and an openness to new ideas and perspectives. While the beliefs of others can provide guidance and inspiration, it is important to remember that your spiritual journey is yours alone. By exploring your own beliefs and values, you can develop a deeper understanding of yourself and the world around you. So, be courageous in your pursuit of spirituality and allow your heart and soul to guide you on this incredible adventure.

Do not wait for the 'perfect' moment to start your spiritual journey; begin right where you are

Each of us has the potential to develop and nurture positive character traits that make us unique. Whether it's our ability to show empathy and compassion towards others, our sense of humour that brings joy to those around us, or our discipline and commitment to achieving our goals, these qualities can help shape our journey towards greater spiritual understanding. Even in the face of challenges such as illness, loss or rejection, we can use them as opportunities to grow and learn. It all starts with taking that first step in the direction that feels right to us and trusting in the journey ahead.

Ask for divine guidance!

When we are feeling lost or overwhelmed, it is easy to feel like we are all alone in the world. But the truth is that we are never truly alone. Whether you believe in a higher power or not, there is always a source of guidance and support available to us if we are willing to ask for it.

If you do believe in a higher power, then asking for divine guidance can be a powerful way to connect with that power and tap into its wisdom and guidance. But even if you don't believe in God or a higher power, the act of asking for help can still be incredibly valuable.

When we ask for guidance, we are essentially acknowledging that we do not have all the answers and that we need help. This can be a humbling experience, but it can also be incredibly empowering. By acknowledging our limitations and asking for help, we open ourselves up to new possibilities and perspectives that we may not have considered before.

So, if you are feeling lost or overwhelmed, do not be afraid to reach out and ask for help. Whether you are asking the universe, your inner wisdom, or a higher power, there is always an answer waiting for you if you are willing to listen. And who knows, you may just find that the guidance you were seeking was within you all along.

Keep on practicing!

Spiritual growth is not a one-time event; it is a lifelong journey that demands consistent practice and effort. Just like any other aspect of life, the path to spiritual enlightenment may have obstacles, setbacks and challenges. But the key is to keep moving forward and not to give up on the journey.

If you are struggling with your spiritual practice, don't be discouraged. Instead, try new approaches and methods to find what works for you. Remember, everyone's journey is different, and what works for one person may not work for another.

Ultimately, the journey to spiritual growth requires dedication, perseverance and effort. It is not always easy, but the rewards are priceless and enduring. So, keep practicing, exploring and learning, for the journey itself is just as important as reaching the destination. By staying committed to the journey, you will discover new insights, perspectives and a deeper sense of inner peace and fulfilment.

Don't worry if your questions remain unanswered!

We live in a world where we crave answers and seek to understand everything that surrounds us. However, we often forget that not everything can be explained, and not every question can be answered. It is in these moments that we must learn to embrace the beauty of unanswered questions without fear.

Unanswered questions possess the power to ignite our curiosity and keep us on a journey of discovery. They challenge us to think beyond our limitations and inspire us to explore new horizons. Yet, despite their importance, many are discouraged and abandon the pursuit of the unknown. They fear what they do not understand and cling to the safety of familiarity.

However, we should not let the unknown deter us from exploring the depths of our spirituality. We should not be afraid to question our beliefs, our values, and our existence. Instead, we should view unanswered questions as an opportunity to grow and expand our consciousness.

It would be quite presumptuous to assume that our limited human minds could unravel all the enigmatic wonders of the universe. We must accept that there are some things we may never understand, and that is okay. We should not let our fear of the unknown prevent us from discovering the hidden treasures of life.

Beware of 'Everyone is Right' thinking

Beware of falling into the trap of believing that everyone is right about the concept of God. Either there is a specific God or there isn't. The notion that God can be moulded to fit an individual's perception is fragile and self-defeating. God is a fixed entity, and it is our duty to diligently seek Him out. So, instead of conforming to popular beliefs, let us take up the challenge and embark on an exciting journey to discover the true nature of God.

❑

CHAPTER 1

Introduction to Spirituality

Spirituality is a personal journey that we all undertake, but it also has a collective essence that connects us all. It is about seeking purpose, meaning and direction in life, and it can take many different forms depending on an individual's beliefs, values and experiences. The allure of spirituality is strong, and it draws people in for various reasons, whether it is to find answers to the most profound questions about life, to look for healing, self-improvement or spiritual growth.

With so much information available online, it is easy to get consumed and confused about what spirituality truly entails. Some may mistake it for religion, while others may see it as a New Age trend. However, spirituality is a broad and complex concept that encompasses all aspects of human experience, from the physical to the emotional, mental and spiritual dimensions of life.

At its core, spirituality is about developing a deep and meaningful relationship with the divine, the universe, or a higher power. It is about connecting with something beyond ourselves and finding inner peace and harmony. It involves exploring and cultivating our inner world, our thoughts, feelings and beliefs, and aligning them with our outer world, our actions, and interactions with others.

In this chapter, let us focus on understanding a comprehensive definition of spirituality and practical insights to guide you on your spiritual journey. Whether you are just starting out or have been on the path for a while, you will find valuable information and inspiration to help you deepen your understanding and experience of spirituality. So, fasten your seat belts, and get ready for an enlightening ride!

Definition of Spirituality

It is fascinating to note that in Sanskrit, spirituality is known as *Adhyātma*, which translates to 'understanding the nature of the soul and one's journey back to identifying with it'. Our natural state is to be blissful, and deep down, we all inherently yearn to be in this state. However, with the stress and strain of modern-day living, happiness can be elusive and fleeting. That is where the expansive science of spirituality comes in—it teaches us how to be blissful!

But spirituality is not just about finding happiness. It encompasses profound questions like 'who am I' and 'what is the purpose of life?' In fact, the sages or those wiser than us, also call it 'supreme science'. It contains all the knowledge and memory of the past, present and future, from the beginning to the end of the universe.

So, while some may think science and spirituality are two separate disciplines, spirituality is actually the knowledge of infinity. It covers everything from the physical world to the subtle unseen world and all living and non-living beings in the universe. Spirituality offers a holistic approach to understanding ourselves and the world around us. It invites us to explore our innermost thoughts and feelings, cultivate mindfulness and self-awareness, and connect with something greater than ourselves.

At its core, spirituality is a transformative journey that encourages us to tap into our inner wisdom and intuition, overcome our limitations and fears, and experience the fullness of life. It offers a path to enlightenment and ultimate liberation from the cycle of birth and death. So, let's embrace this supreme science of spirituality and embark on a journey of self-discovery, growth and evolution.

Why is spirituality important to us?

The desire for happiness is universal, and it drives us in all our endeavours. Yet, studies have shown that on average, people only experience happiness 30 per cent of the time. Why is this so? While we all know about the physical and psychological causes of life's problems, what many fail to realise is that these issues can often have a spiritual root cause. Shockingly, over 50 per cent of the problems we face in life are due to spiritual reasons.

This means that even if a problem manifests as a physical or psychological issue, its root cause may be of a spiritual nature. Therefore, seeking spiritual solutions can provide relief not only to physical and psychological symptoms but also to the underlying spiritual cause. The practice of spirituality offers a unique approach to resolving life's challenges by addressing the root cause of problems and not just their symptoms.

By exploring the spiritual realm, we can gain deeper insights into the nature of reality, ourselves, and our connection to the divine. Spirituality offers a way to tap into a higher power and access a source of wisdom and guidance beyond our limited understanding. It can help us develop a greater sense of purpose and meaning in life and guide us towards the path of true and lasting happiness.

Moreover, spirituality teaches us to cultivate virtues such as compassion, gratitude, forgiveness and love, which not only benefit ourselves but also those around us. It helps us develop a positive outlook towards life and the world, leading to a greater sense of inner peace and harmony.

In conclusion, if you want to experience true and lasting happiness, it might be worth exploring the spiritual realm for answers. By addressing the root cause of life's problems through spirituality, we can cultivate a deeper sense of meaning and purpose in life, leading to a more fulfilling and joyful existence.

Spirituality and the purpose of life

As we navigate through the ups and downs of life, it is natural to wonder about the bigger picture and what all it means. Is there a purpose to our existence, or are we simply a product of chance? The pursuit of material possessions and success may bring temporary happiness, but deep down, we all yearn for something more meaningful and lasting. This is where spirituality comes in—it provides a framework for exploring the deeper questions of life and discovering our true purpose.

By understanding the laws of the universe and our place within it, we can learn to live in harmony with ourselves and the world around us. This not only leads to greater fulfilment and happiness in life but also helps us fulfil our destiny and attain spiritual growth. Through spiritual practices such as meditation, selfless service and introspection, we can cultivate a deeper understanding of our true nature and our relationship with the divine. So, if you are feeling confused, directionless or unfulfilled in life, consider exploring the realm of spirituality. Who knows, it may lead you to discover your true purpose and unlock a deeper sense of meaning and happiness in life.

Obstacles in spirituality

Embarking on a spiritual journey can be a daunting task, and there are bound to be challenges along the way. However, with the right mindset and tools, these challenges can be overcome. Surrounding yourself with a supportive community can help keep you on track and provide the necessary motivation when you feel like giving up. It is also crucial to be discerning in choosing a spiritual mentor or guide, as they can be the difference between progressing towards your goals or being led astray. Moreover, being aware of your own doubts and negative energies can prevent them from becoming roadblocks to your spiritual growth.

Spiritual practices such as meditation, mindfulness and self-reflection can help you develop this awareness and create a strong foundation for your spiritual journey. Above all, remember that spirituality is a personal journey, and everyone's path may differ. So, embrace the journey and trust the process, and you will inevitably reach your destination of connecting with your higher self.

❑

CHAPTER 2

Why be a Spiritual Person?

Spirituality is a concept that transcends religion and conflicts, uniting people all over the world under the common goal of achieving inner peace, connecting with the higher self and enlightenment, of course. A spiritually mature person understands the interconnectedness of all living beings and accepts them without judgement or the desire to change them. They work towards universal welfare, without seeking approval or expecting anything in return. They are content with their actions, guided by a higher purpose, and free from the need to compare themselves to others.

Spirituality is not about earthly gains or losses, but about finding a state of equanimity beyond duality. When we reach this sublime state, the dualities of good and bad, profit and loss, and sorrow and happiness, lose their significance. As a result, spiritual people experience a deep sense of joy and contentment that surpasses any material pleasure.

The benefits of spirituality are immense and far-reaching. Regardless of what one desires or asks for, the higher power will ensure that the benefits adapt themselves to the individual's needs. Moreover, the benefits start flowing in during the very process of becoming spiritual and not just after achieving enlightenment.

The path to spirituality is intricate, and sometimes, seekers may encounter obstacles and challenges that make them question their journey. However, the effort put into spiritual growth is never wasted, and even if this life ends abruptly, the noble qualities and capabilities developed during this process continue to remain alive and vibrant in their next incarnation.

Striving for spiritual growth helps us overcome evil and leads us towards good, where our highest goal is to be loving to ourselves and others.

In conclusion, the journey towards spirituality is not an easy one, but it is a rewarding one. By cultivating a spiritual mindset and following universal principles, we can achieve inner peace and contentment, and work towards universal welfare, making the world a better place for ourselves and others.

What are the uses of spirituality?

Spirituality can be a powerful force in the lives of those seeking a deeper understanding of their place in the world.

It offers a means to explore existential questions about the meaning of life and the nature of reality. Whether through organised religion, personal introspection, or a combination of both, spirituality can provide individuals with the tools to navigate life's challenges and find peace and solace in times of stress, depression and anxiety.

Finding purpose and meaning

One of the most compelling reasons people turn to spirituality is to find purpose and meaning. Many find that traditional religious practices or spiritual pursuits can offer a sense of direction and clarity that is difficult to find elsewhere. By exploring spiritual texts, engaging in rituals and practices, or simply reflecting on their own experiences and beliefs, individuals can gain a deeper understanding of their own values, priorities and goals. This can lead to a greater sense of purpose and a more fulfilling life.

Coping with difficult emotions and experiences

Spirituality can also serve as a means of coping with difficult emotions and experiences. By fostering a connection to a higher power or universal force, individuals can find comfort and hope in times of hardship. This can be especially important for those struggling with mental health issues, as spirituality can offer an alternative or complementary approach to traditional therapy and medication.

Community and social support

In addition to these personal benefits, spirituality can also provide a sense of community and social support. Spiritual communities and organised religions often offer opportunities for fellowship, service and collective worship. This can be a valuable source of connection and support for those seeking to share their spiritual journey with like-minded individuals.

Meaningful path towards self-growth

Regardless of one's beliefs or religious affiliation, exploring spirituality can provide a meaningful path towards personal growth, self-discovery, and a greater sense of purpose. By cultivating a deeper understanding of themselves and the world around them, individuals can lead more fulfilling lives and contribute positively to the world around them.

What are the benefits of spirituality?

Spiritual wellness is an essential part of our overall health and well-being. It involves developing a deeper understanding of ourselves and the world around us through spiritual practices such as meditation, prayer and reflection. When we prioritise spiritual wellness, we can experience a host of benefits that enrich our lives and enhance our sense of purpose.

Enhanced spiritual growth and understanding

One of the key advantages of spiritual wellness is the potential for enhanced spiritual growth and understanding. By engaging in practices that connect us to something greater than ourselves, we can gain new insights and perspectives that help us navigate life's challenges with greater clarity and wisdom.

Greater peace and calmness

Another benefit of spiritual wellness is the potential for greater peace and calmness in our lives. By tapping into our spiritual side, we can access a sense of tranquillity that helps us manage stress and anxiety more effectively. This can lead to a greater sense of balance and harmony in our daily lives.

Leading to a more meaningful life

Spiritual wellness can also help us lead more meaningful lives. By aligning our passions and interests with our spiritual values, such as kindness and generosity, we can find greater fulfilment and purpose in our daily pursuits.

Foster a sense of connection

Spiritual wellness can foster a sense of connection to a larger community. By seeking out like-minded individuals who share our spiritual values, we can create a sense of camaraderie and support that enhances our overall well-being.

Improved physical health and better relationships

In addition to these benefits, spiritual wellness can also lead to improved physical health and better relationships. By managing stress more effectively and adopting healthier lifestyle habits, we can improve our physical health. And by cultivating greater compassion and understanding through spiritual practices, we can enhance our relationships and foster deeper connections with others.

In short, spiritual wellness offers a range of benefits that can enrich our lives and enhance our overall health and well-being. By prioritising our spiritual growth and development, we can lead more fulfilling and purposeful lives, and contribute positively to the world around us.

What is the impact of spirituality?

Spirituality has long been a source of comfort and solace for individuals seeking meaning and purpose in life. It can have a transformative impact on our lives, influencing our thoughts, beliefs and actions in profound ways. At its core, spirituality is about connecting with a higher power or consciousness, transcending the limitations of the ego, and finding greater meaning and purpose in life.

While the specific beliefs and practices may vary, research has shown that engaging in spiritual activity can have numerous positive effects on mental and physical health. One of the most significant impacts of spirituality is that it can help us see the world in a more positive light. This is because when we are in tune with our spiritual selves, we tend to focus on the positive aspects of life rather than the negative. In a sense, it is like the algorithm on social media platforms—the more we engage with positive content, the more the algorithm shows us similar content. Similarly, when we cultivate a positive and spiritual outlook on life, the universe seems to respond by presenting us with more positive experiences and opportunities.

But the benefits don't end here. Research has linked prayer and spirituality to better health, greater psychological well-being, and even superior stress management skills during challenging times. It is no wonder that spirituality has become a popular coping mechanism for individuals of all ages looking to improve their overall well-being.

Spirituality can also help us cultivate greater inner peace and harmony. When we practice spiritual techniques such as meditation, prayer and mindfulness, we learn to quiet the mind and tune in to our inner selves. This can help us reduce stress and anxiety, improve our emotional well-being, and foster greater feelings of contentment and happiness.

In addition, spirituality can help us find greater purpose and direction in life. When we connect with a higher power or consciousness, we gain a deeper understanding of our place in the world and our unique gifts and talents. This can inspire us to pursue our passions and make a positive impact on the world around us.

Overall, the impact of spirituality is far-reaching and can transform every aspect of our lives. By seeing the world in a more positive light, cultivating inner peace and harmony, and finding greater purpose and direction, we can create a more fulfilling and meaningful life.

What can be the potential pitfalls?

While spirituality can be a powerful tool for growth and self-improvement, it's important to be aware of its potential pitfalls. One such pitfall is known as spiritual bypassing, where individuals use spirituality as a means of avoiding real-world problems, conflicts or emotions. Instead of addressing the root cause of an issue or taking responsibility for their actions, they may use spiritual platitudes as a means to sidestep the problem altogether. However, this approach can ultimately lead to a lack of empathy, dogmatism and a failure to address the needs of others. To avoid this trap, it's important to approach spirituality with mindfulness and balance, recognising that while it can offer profound insights, it's not a substitute for taking action in the real world.

An example of spiritual bypassing in action could be a person who is struggling with a difficult relationship and instead of taking active steps to address the underlying issues, they retreat into a spiritual practice. They may use mantras or affirmations to try and manifest a better relationship or justify the problems in their relationship by believing it is a 'lesson' that they need to learn to grow spiritually. While spiritual practices can be helpful in dealing with emotions and conflicts, in this case, it may serve to avoid taking responsibility for their own actions and communication patterns within the relationship.

By using spirituality to avoid the real-world issues at hand, the person may neglect to address the underlying problems in their relationship, leading to further conflicts and emotional distress. It is important to recognise that while spiritual practices can be powerful tools for growth and transformation, they are not a substitute for real-world action and problem-solving. By approaching spirituality with mindfulness and balance, we can use it as a tool for personal growth while also recognising the importance of acting in the real world.

How spirituality can be practiced?

Have you ever felt the need to reconnect with your spiritual side, but didn't know where to start? Well, the good news is that there are plenty of ways to begin your journey towards a more spiritually fulfilling life. Whether you are looking to rediscover an old path or explore a new one, incorporating spirituality into your daily routine has been shown to have a positive impact on your well-being.

While everyone's spiritual journey is unique, research suggests that there are some universal strategies that can help to reduce stress and promote a more mindful approach to life. Here are some tips to get you started:

- First, **tune in to your emotions**: Embracing spirituality means acknowledging the full range of human experience, from the highs to the lows.
- Next, **focus on others**: Cultivating empathy and kindness towards others is a core tenet of many spiritual practices.
- **Meditation** can also be a powerful tool for spiritual growth. Just 10-15 minutes of daily meditation can help to calm your mind and connect you with your inner self.
- Another strategy is to **practice gratitude**. By keeping a journal and jotting down what you are thankful for each day, you can develop a greater appreciation for life's blessings and cultivate a positive outlook.
- Finally, try **incorporating mindfulness** into your daily routine. This involves staying present in the moment, without judgement or distraction, and can help you find greater peace and clarity in your day-to-day life.

❑

CHAPTER 3

Signs You are a Spiritual Person!

Are you really a spiritual person?

Spirituality can be a transformative state of mind, bringing a sense of purpose, meaning and direction to life. It allows you to rise above the mundane and connect with something greater than yourself. If you feel a deep sense of peace and harmony within yourself and find yourself less affected by the ups and downs of daily life, you may be on the path to spirituality. Other signs include a growing sense of compassion and empathy for others, a desire to live a more purposeful life, and an appreciation for the beauty and wonder of the world around you. By cultivating these qualities, you can continue to deepen your spiritual journey and experience even greater peace and fulfilment.

You avoid gossiping

When you no longer find pleasure in speaking ill of others or engaging in gossip, it could be a sign of a heightened spiritual state. Instead, you strive to see the best in people and are averse to negativity. Criticising or judging others may provoke feelings of frustration or annoyance in you, as you aspire to create a space for positivity and kindness in your life.

Nothing scares you!

If you have reached a point where you are no longer fearful of life's challenges, and instead embrace them with an open heart and mind, then you may be on the path towards spirituality. This involves letting go of the things that once scared you, such as rejection, loneliness and failure, and focusing on the positive aspects of life. By doing so, you can achieve a deep sense of peace and fulfilment that comes from within and experience a greater sense of harmony among your body, mind and soul.

Kindness is something you prioritise

One of the most prominent signs of a spiritual person is their constant state of joy and kindness towards others. Rather than engaging in negative behaviours like criticism or judgement, they strive to uplift and encourage those around them, with the ultimate goal of making the world a better place. If you find that you share these values and make an effort to spread positivity, then you may very well be on a spiritual path.

You like to acquire knowledge

If you are driven by a deep desire to acquire knowledge and to achieve your goals, then you are likely on a spiritual path. This is not a mere thirst for textbook knowledge or material wealth, but a profound curiosity about the world, emotions and spiritual processes. You are constantly seeking to learn and grow, and you regularly take time to reflect on your inner self through introspection. Your dedication to personal growth and enlightenment is a sure sign that you are embracing your spirituality.

Meditation helps you acquire inner peace

Meditation can be a powerful tool on the path to spirituality, but it requires patience and practice. Not everyone can meditate for an extended period of time, but it is recommended to aim for at least 5 to 10 minutes. As you deepen your spiritual practice, you may find that meditation becomes a source of inner peace and happiness. It can elevate your consciousness and bring a sense of tranquility to your mind, body, and soul.

Twenty powerful signs that you are spiritually healthy:

1. You have taken control of your life and are intentionally living the life you want to—creating and achieving life goals.
2. You are living a life that aligns with your soul's purpose and you love it.
3. You feel fulfilled by giving back to your community with a generous spirit.
4. You have achieved emotional stability and your moods are steady.
5. You are aware of your own biases and do not judge others based on them.
6. You do not fear making mistakes because you see them as opportunities to learn and grow.
7. You understand that true freedom and happiness come from within and work to cultivate them.
8. You are confident in being your authentic self, both personally and professionally.
9. You prioritise daily moments of silence and stillness.
10. You are not afraid to let go of relationships that no longer serve you.
11. You make time for playful and imaginative activities every day.

12. You enjoy being alone and appreciate the peace it brings.
13. You have a heightened sense of awareness and appreciation for beauty and detail.
14. You confidently express your needs and desires.
15. You do not feel the need to explain yourself to others.
16. You are able to stay present and in the moment without distraction.
17. You trust your intuition and act on it without hesitation.
18. You view problems as opportunities for growth and learning.
19. You are open to falling in love with different aspects of life repeatedly.
20. You begin and end each day with a good intention and gratitude.

Five signs of spiritual growth

When it comes to personal growth, there are plenty of obvious signs of progress—money, success and family growth, for example. However, there is one type of growth that goes unnoticed, hidden beneath the surface, and that is spiritual growth. In fact, even someone who has achieved spiritual enlightenment cannot be recognised by their outward appearance.

This may sound mystical, but it is not meant to discourage those on the spiritual path. The reason spiritual growth is unseen is that it only happens within consciousness. You cannot just think your way to a higher spiritual state. Instead, it requires an understanding of how consciousness works. As an ancient Indian saying goes, 'Know this one thing by which all else is known'.

In our daily lives, we are constantly guided by mental activity, whether it is new desires, fears, habits or random thoughts. However, not all this mental activity is relevant to spiritual growth. Positive and negative thoughts can impact our daily lives, but they do not affect our state of awareness, which is the key focus for spiritual growth. So, if you are looking to grow spiritually, remember that it's the unseen, internal changes that matter most.

Sign 1: Consciousness is the source of creation

At the core of existence lies consciousness, the very foundation from which all things spring forth into being. Regardless of cultural or spiritual background, all traditions recognise this fundamental truth: the wellspring of creation is rooted in a state of awareness. This hidden force, which lies beyond our perception, envelops and sustains each and every one of us, providing a context for our individual consciousness to flourish within.

Sign 2: The spiritual path is transcendent

Discovering your source of inner wisdom does not require complex rituals, convoluted philosophies, or intense emotional experiences. All it takes is the power of simple awareness. By quieting the mental chatter and finding inner stillness, you can tap into a wellspring of calm and centredness that lies within you.

While traditional meditation can be challenging in our fast-paced modern world, there are still ways to cultivate this state of mind. Simply find a quiet place, take a few deep breaths, and focus on your breathing with eyes closed. Regular practice of this centering exercise throughout the day will help you become more familiar with the sensation of simple awareness, allowing your mind to let go of constant distractions and become more attuned to deeper levels of consciousness.

Sign 3: True self is the deeper level of awareness

The spiritual journey may seem daunting, but it all begins with a single step: simple awareness. While the ultimate goal of enlightenment may seem distant and unattainable, there are many milestones along the way that can bring us closer to our true selves

These milestones are the experiences of higher consciousness that we encounter every day, although we may not always recognise them as such. Love, compassion, empathy, beauty, truth, creativity, insight and bliss are all glimpses of our true selves, and by paying attention to these moments, we can begin to understand our innermost nature.

So don't be discouraged by the enormity of the spiritual path. Start by noticing the moments of higher consciousness that already exist within you and let them guide you towards a deeper understanding of your true self.

Sign 4: Your level of awareness depends upon the values you favour

Have you ever experienced a moment of pure beauty, love or insight that left you feeling truly alive? These glimpses of your true self or higher consciousness are more common than you might think, but to truly grow spiritually, you need to pay attention to them.

Think of these fleeting moments as doorways to a deeper understanding of yourself and the world around you. To step through that doorway and leave behind the noise and distractions of everyday life, there are three simple steps you can take:

First, take a moment to notice the experience and allow it to sink in. Let it become your sole focus, even if just for a brief moment.

Next, value and savour the experience by offering gratitude and appreciation from the heart. This creates a warm bond between you and the moment of higher consciousness, opening up a deeper connection to your true self.

Finally, follow where the experience leads. Within every glimpse of the true self lies a hint of bliss, joy and ecstasy that can guide you towards your true calling and the life you were meant to live. By following your bliss, you can confidently navigate the path towards your higher self and the spiritual growth you seek.

Sign 5: Creative intelligence is aligning everything

The true self is like a radio station broadcasting a constant stream of messages. However, our everyday mind can be like a faulty receiver, making it hard to tune in and follow these messages. But the more we align ourselves with our true self, the clearer the signal becomes, revealing the life we are meant to live.

This life, or Dharma, is not a predetermined destiny or a set of rules to follow. Instead, it is a stream of desires that naturally arise from within, leading us towards our true self. This means that the spiritual path is a path of desire, where each step brings fulfilment and joy, and resistance is easily cleared away.

To find your Dharma, pay attention to what brings you inner contentment and a sense of purpose. When you feel in the groove and things come easily, you are aligned with your true self. By following your vision and desires, you can experience a life filled with bliss and meaning.

While this may not be the experience of everyone, the choice to transform and change is always available. By embracing our desires and following the path of bliss, we can uncover our Dharma and experience spiritual growth in a fulfilling and joyful way.

❑

CHAPTER 4

What is the Difference Between Religion and Spirituality?

Since the dawn of civilisation, humans have been entranced by the mystical realm and the greater purpose of existence. From the earliest times, spiritual guides like sages and seers have helped people navigate their spiritual paths, leading to the emergence of religions with their intricate tales and archetypes. Yet, even with these rich belief systems, some individuals still needed to be fulfilled, seeking a deeper connection to the divine.

Among these seekers was Gautama Buddha, who refused to accept religion's ready-made answers and embarked on his quest for spiritual truth. This search for authenticity and a direct experience of spiritual awakening has persisted throughout history, drawing countless individuals towards spirituality and away from traditional religious institutions. So, whether through established religion or a personal spiritual journey, pursuing the divine continues to captivate our hearts and minds as we seek to uncover the mysteries of the universe and our place in it.

Why is it important to distinguish between religion and spirituality?

Although religion and spirituality pose many common questions, the answers they offer are often worlds apart. Religion provides predetermined answers that are widely accepted, whereas spirituality is a personal journey of discovery. Before we explore why it's crucial to differentiate between the two, let's first define each of these paths to enlightenment.

What is Religion?

Religion is a complex and multifaceted aspect of human society, encompassing a wide range of beliefs, practices and traditions. It has the power to inspire and unify, bringing people together around shared values and common goals. For many, religion provides a sense of purpose, direction and moral guidance, helping them navigate the complexities of life. At the same time, it can also be a source of controversy and conflict, as different interpretations and beliefs clash. Despite its complexities, religion remains an important and influential part of our world, shaping our societies and communities in countless ways.

What is spirituality?

Spirituality is a personal quest for a higher connection with the divine and understanding our place in the universe. It does not necessarily involve strict dogmas or beliefs that remain unchanged. Instead, spiritual ideas can evolve and grow through personal experiences and introspection. People can draw inspiration from existing religions or forge their path toward enlightenment.

Although spirituality and religion share some common threads, they differ significantly in many ways. It's crucial to distinguish between them to define one's journey. As more people become disillusioned with established traditions, the debate between spirituality and religion has gained momentum. Many now identify as spiritual but not religious, seeking transcendental answers that align with their unique perspectives and choices in life.

Spirituality offers a path of self-discovery and personal growth, while religion often provides a structured system of beliefs and practices. Both can coexist, but the choice of which to follow is ultimately a deeply personal. So, whether you are a spiritual seeker, a religious devotee, or somewhere in between, the quest for meaning and purpose remains an essential part of the human experience.

How are religion and spirituality alike?

Religion and spirituality share fundamental characteristics that make them more than just words we toss around in everyday conversations. Both concepts are defined by the presence of the sacred, which give them a deeper meaning than other psychological terms like well-being or hope.

Moreover, religion and spirituality are journeys of discovery and transformation that can change over time. They can take many forms, from personal reflections to group practices, and are expressed in various settings, from individual experiences to cultural traditions.

However, like most things in life, religion and spirituality can have positive and negative effects. While they offer significant value to individuals and communities, they can also be a source of conflict and division.

Ultimately, what matters most is the pursuit of something greater than us. Whether it's the search for a sacred destination or the purpose of significant goals, religion and spirituality offer a way to connect with the profound aspects of life. And when faith is focused on the sacred, it becomes virtually indistinguishable from spirituality. So, whether you choose to follow a religious or spiritual path, the journey matters most.

Differences between religion and spirituality

Religion and spirituality are often confused as interchangeable terms, but they are fundamentally different concepts. Religion is a set of organised beliefs, practices and rituals that are shared by a community of people. Spirituality, on the other hand, is a personal journey towards self-discovery, inner peace, and connection with a higher power.

One of the most significant differences between religion and spirituality is the communal versus personal aspect of faith. Religion is a communal affair that involves shared beliefs, practices and values within a particular group. In contrast, spirituality is a deeply personal journey that can be undertaken independently or with guidance from others.

Religion is taught, while spirituality is discovered. Religion has a set of predetermined paths, while spirituality is an internal discovery that stems from a significant event that triggers one to question their existence and seek higher purpose.

Furthermore, religion often has strict codes of conduct and a dogmatic approach to adhering to certain beliefs. In contrast, spirituality encourages exploration beyond traditional boundaries, allows for differing perspectives, and is open to personal growth and change.

Religion is focused on future rewards, while spirituality emphasises living in the present and experiencing life as it happens. Religion is highly organised, while spirituality is adaptable and can develop naturally with the individual. Religion places emphasis on tradition, while spirituality is organic and develops over time.

Religion may be exclusive and may follow a particular belief system, while spirituality is inclusive and allows individuals to draw from various belief systems.

In conclusion, while both religion and spirituality offer unique ways to connect with a higher power, it is essential to recognise their differences. Spirituality offers a personal journey of self-discovery, inner peace, and growth that can adapt and evolve with an individual's needs. Religion, on the other hand, offers a communal belief system that can provide structure and a sense of belonging but may also be restrictive and exclusive. Ultimately, the choice of whether to pursue a religious or spiritual path is a personal one that should be approached with an open mind and heart.

What is 'spiritual but not religious'?

Are you seeking a higher purpose in life, but do not identify with any religion? Then you may fall into the category of being 'spiritual but not religious'. This label applies to individuals who continue to develop themselves spiritually without adhering to the beliefs and practices of a specific religious tradition. It includes those who were once religious but have since abandoned it, as well as those who have never been religious but still seek a deeper understanding of the world around them.

❑

CHAPTER 5

Types of Spirituality

In the realm of spirituality, there are various types of belief systems ranging from heart-centred to dogmatic to intellectual, and sometimes a combination of these. The beauty of spirituality lies in the fact that it acknowledges that there are multiple paths leading to the same destination, and no one way is more superior than another. It is a personal journey that one takes, and while others may offer guidance, the experience is ultimately a solo one. Spirituality also recognises a higher power that connects all of us, extending beyond our earthly existence, making it a profound and enlightening journey.

There are three types of spirituality mindsets:

1. Dogmatic spirituality

Dogmatic spirituality imposes strict rules, and often requires adherence to a specific set of leaders and teachers. Those who follow dogmatic spirituality tend to believe that their way is the only way and can be dismissive of other beliefs or practices. For instance, they might insist that only one form of meditation or prayer is valid, or that spiritual growth must adhere to a particular path.

While dogmatic spirituality can offer a sense of structure and guidance, it can also lead to rigid thinking and a lack of openness to new ideas. On the other hand, some people may find solace in dogmatic spirituality during times of uncertainty, as it can provide a clear sense of direction and purpose. Ultimately, the choice of whether to follow a dogmatic or more flexible spiritual path is a deeply personal one.

2. Heart-centred spirituality

Have you ever felt like the outside world reflects your inner world? Well, that's the foundation of heart-centred spirituality. It's all about self-reflection and self-love, where your inner state affects your outer reality. And it's not just about you; this spiritual mindset also believes that we are all connected, so our collective joy and suffering impact the world.

Heart-centred spirituality encourages us to let go of control and allows energy to flow freely, instead of trying to control everything and everyone around us. This spiritual mindset empowers us to observe and understand our emotions, so we can tap into our inner power and create a more joyful world.

3. Intellectual spirituality

Are you the kind of person who loves to expand your knowledge and learn new things? If so, intellectual spirituality might be right up your alley! As a seeker on this path, you will dive into fascinating theories and practices, all while prioritising your understanding of them over the actual experience. It's a stimulating and exciting journey, perfect for those who crave mental challenges and growth.

What are the pillars of spiritual living?

Are you looking to live a more fulfilled and meaningful life? Incorporating spirituality into your daily routine can have positive effects on your mental, physical and emotional health. In this practice, service, and community-based approach to wellness, we will explore ways to prioritise your spiritual practice, bring kindness into your life, foster a strong social support system, and even introduce a new and improved version of the golden rule. By embracing these practices, you can unlock a world of possibilities and experience a richer, more meaningful spiritual life while also boosting your overall well-being.

Pillar 1

Practice: Wake up to wellness

Do you want to live a fulfilled spiritual life? Starting your day with techniques like kundalini yoga, Chi Gong, deep relaxation, meditation, or prayer can have positive effects on your mental, physical and emotional health. Research shows that meditation can activate and calm different parts of the brain, making it an excellent tool for spiritual growth. Developing a regular morning practice, known as *sadhana*, is a historical tradition for achieving health, happiness, and spiritual fulfilment. As one master wisely said, "You can do anything you want after *sadhana*." So why not prioritise your spiritual practice and unlock a world of possibilities?

Pillar 2

Service: Bring kindness into your life

Did you know that serving others, even with small acts like offering a smile or a silent prayer, can reduce your own stress levels? This is supported by research which shows that compassionate and altruistic behaviours can have a positive impact on our physical and mental health. Scientists have found that such acts can lower the levels of cortisol, the stress hormone, and boost the function of the immune system. So, the next time you're feeling stressed, try offering a helping hand to someone in need and see how it can benefit both of you!

Pillar 3

Community: Foster a strong social support system

Both Eastern healing philosophy and Western science agree that the energy of the group, whether it's from family, friends, or members of a religious organisation, has a significant impact on our well-being. It's crucial to surround yourself with people who uplift and support your energy, as opposed to those who drain it, if you want to feel fantastic.

Pillar 4

Remember: Don't forget the new golden rule

We all know the adage: 'Do unto others as you would have them do unto you', but there's a new and improved version: 'See the other person as yourself. See the other person as a soul'. This means acknowledging that every person you meet carries a spark of the divine inside, just like you do.

When you start to see others as extensions of yourself, your interactions become more loving, intimate and unified. This simple shift in perspective can lead to enlightenment and a richer, more meaningful spiritual life. Plus, research shows that living a spiritual lifestyle can also boost your physical and mental health.

❑

CHAPTER 6

How to Get in Touch with Your Spiritual Side?

The road to achieving the life of your dreams is paved with good intentions, but it's not always smooth sailing. Despite your best efforts, challenges may arise that cause you to lose focus and put off personal growth and healing for another day. When the call to begin or deepen your spiritual journey arises, the question that often comes to mind is 'Where do I start?' The process of figuring out how to begin and maintain a spiritual practice can be daunting and may trigger feelings of anxiety, especially if you are a novice in this area.

As someone who has experienced false starts and long breaks in my own spiritual journey, I've discovered that the key to making progress is to establish a daily spiritual practice. In simple terms, a daily spiritual practice is a routine of activities that you perform each day to support your personal evolution. To ensure maximum benefit, it's essential to incorporate practices that address the four essential categories of your life: physical, emotional, mental and spiritual.

By consistently dedicating time to your spiritual practice, you will be able to maintain and improve all areas of your life, both major and subtle.

So, if you are ready to take the first step towards your spiritual journey, let's dive in and explore these simple steps for building a daily spiritual practice that will help you achieve the life of your dreams!

1. Pick your practice

To ensure the success of your daily spiritual practice, it's essential to establish a structure that will support your efforts. The first step is to make a list of at least four activities that you can do every day to nurture your highest self, keeping in mind the four categories of physical, emotional, mental and spiritual well-being.

You can choose from a variety of options, including meditation, yoga, affirmations, smudging, prayer, reading uplifting material, working with crystals, journaling, spending time in nature, expressing gratitude, engaging in self-praise, and practicing breathwork exercises. You are free to add anything that resonates with you, and it is okay to experiment until you find what works best for you.

Once you have chosen your daily activities, the next step is to structure your time. Ideally, daily practices work best when experienced at the start of your day, so decide on the minimum and maximum amount of time you are willing to dedicate to your routine each morning. It's essential to be honest with yourself and set realistic expectations. Will you spend 15 minutes, 45 minutes or 2 hours on your practice? The key is to commit to a routine that you can sustain and maintain over time.

To help stay on track, it can be beneficial to develop two versions of your daily practice. One that you can do in 15 minutes if you are short on time, and a more extensive version that lasts for 45 to 60 minutes on days when you have more flexibility. This way, you can adapt your routine to fit your schedule without sacrificing the quality of your practice.

In summary, establishing a daily spiritual practice is a powerful way to nurture your personal growth and well-being. By creating a structure and committing to consistent efforts, you can cultivate a deeper connection with your highest self and experience profound transformation in all areas of your life.

2. It's time to create a space

As you embark on your journey of spiritual growth, it's important to create a designated space in your home that serves as a sanctuary for your daily practice. This sacred space should be a private area, whether it's a small corner, a cosy nook, a garage or a den, where you can retreat every morning to connect with your highest self.

When designing your sacred space, feel free to let your creative juices flow! Consider incorporating items that speak to your soul and help cultivate a peaceful, uplifting atmosphere. For instance, candles can infuse the space with warm light and comforting scents, while journals and spiritual books can inspire and guide you on your journey. Meaningful family heirlooms, photos that make you smile, and sacred objects can remind you of the love and support that surround you. Art, comfortable pillows, and other decor can help create a cosy and inviting ambiance that draws you in.

Make your sacred space uniquely yours by adding your own personal touches, such as your favourite affirmations or essential oils that resonate with you. The goal is to create a space that feels special and inviting, a space where you can feel comfortable being yourself and exploring your spiritual practice.

Remember, this space is yours and yours alone. It should be a place where you feel safe, supported, and inspired to grow and evolve. So, take your time, enjoy the process, and allow yourself to create a space that truly nourishes your soul.

3. Commit

To fully commit to your spiritual growth, it's important to honour your heart's desires and make a conscious decision to put in the effort. This can be done by creating an agreement with yourself and writing out your intentions. Make sure to say them out loud and put them in a visible place, such as a vision board or sticky note, as a reminder of your commitment to yourself.

Your agreement should include specific details such as the frequency and duration of your practice, as well as the areas of your life that you want to improve and heal. By stating your intentions clearly, you are setting yourself up for success and reminding yourself of the importance of consistency.

It's important to remember that committing to your growth is not a one-time event but a continuous process. You may encounter challenges and setbacks along the way, but the key is to stay focused on your intentions and recommit yourself to the process when needed. With consistency, patience and dedication, you can achieve the life of your dreams.

4. Begin NOW!

Today marks the beginning of your journey towards the highest version of yourself. As you embark on this new chapter, it's important to remember that there is no right or wrong way to do this. Simply honour your soul by spending 15-60 minutes going through the routine of your newly created spiritual practice. It's natural for your mind to wander during this time, and that's okay. If it happens, gently release the thoughts and keep going.

To fully immerse yourself in this practice, make sure you schedule enough time for it. Rushing through it defeats the purpose of creating a sacred space for yourself. Remember to be patient and gentle with yourself, as this is a journey and not a race.

As you go through your routine, allow yourself to fully experience each moment. Pay attention to how your body, mind and spirit feel. Take note of the changes, both subtle and significant, that occur as you practice each day.

Finally, remember to repeat this practice daily. Consistency is key when it comes to spiritual growth. Each day brings a new opportunity for you to deepen your connection with your highest self. So, execute your routine with intention, and watch as your life begins to transform in beautiful and unexpected ways.

5. Expand your vision

As you continue to nurture your highest self, it is important to reflect on your progress and adjust as needed. Self-evaluation can be a powerful tool in this journey of self-discovery. Take some time to ask yourself the right questions: How do you feel mentally, spiritually, physically and emotionally? What have you noticed about yourself or your reactions to the world? What areas of your life do you feel in charge of? And what parts of your daily practice do you enjoy the most? What parts feel challenging?

Remember that your practice is unique to you, and it is okay to adjust along the way. Perhaps you have mastered your morning routine and want to add a mini evening practice, such as an Epsom salt bath or setting bedtime intentions. The possibilities are endless!

As you continue to commit to your practice, you will begin to see incredible growth in all areas of your life. You will attract abundance effortlessly, experience deeper connections in your relationships, and feel a sense of lightness and joy in your being. The world will open to you in new and exciting ways. So keep going, trust the process, and know that you are on the path to becoming the best version of yourself!

6. Prayer...prayer...prayer

Prayer is a powerful way to connect with your higher power, whether you believe in God, the universe, or something else entirely. It's a chance to have a conversation with the divine, expressing your gratitude, hopes and fears.

When you wake up in the morning, you can set your intentions for the day with a prayer, asking for guidance and strength to stay sober. At night, you can reflect on the day and give thanks for another day of sobriety. And throughout the day, you can say little prayers of gratitude or ask for help when you need it.

So, just start by finding a quiet place to sit, close your eyes, and let the words flow.

6. Establish a connection with nature

Have you ever felt a spiritual connection to nature? Many people have found that immersing themselves in the natural world can bring them inner peace. From hiking through lush forests to basking in the warmth of the sun on a grassy meadow, there are endless opportunities to connect with nature. You can even find solace in the quiet shade of a tree or escape on a camping trip to marvel at the stars above. So why not explore the healing power of nature and embark on your own spiritual journey?

7. Yoga

Did you know that yoga is an ancient practice that has been around for over 5,000 years? Its deliberate combination of body postures and breathing exercises can work wonders. By bringing together the mind, body and spirit, yoga helps individuals to rediscover themselves and reconnect with their true inner selves. After struggling with substance abuse, many newly sober people experience a profound sense of disconnection. However, practicing yoga can help to rebuild this connection and pave the way towards a more fulfilling and balanced life.

8. Become a part of any spiritual or religious gathering

One of the most fascinating aspects of spirituality is that it allows you to cultivate a personal relationship with a higher power that you connect with on a deep level. You have the freedom to choose any belief system that resonates with you, allowing you to attend any worship service that aligns with your unique spirituality.

Also, attending a religious or spiritual service held in a church, temple, synagogue, mosque or other sacred space, can provide a sense of structure and support. It is also an excellent opportunity to bond with people who share similar beliefs and values, offering a chance for meaningful fellowship and community. So, why not explore the diverse spiritual landscape and find your own path towards a fulfilling and connected life?

9. Meditate

Have you ever heard the saying: 'Prayer is when you talk to God, and meditation is when God talks to you?' While prayer is a way for us to communicate with a higher power, meditation is a way for us to listen and connect with our inner selves.

Many people are intimidated by meditation and the idea of sitting in silence for a prolonged period. It's understandable to feel anxious about the constant chatter in our minds. However, the irony is that regular meditation can reduce mental chatter and provide a multitude of other benefits.

Conclusive words

Scientific research has shown that meditation can boost mood, reduce stress and anxiety, promote restful sleep, and even act as a natural pain reliever. There are various types of meditation, but the general idea is to sit quietly with your eyes closed and focus on your breath. You don't need any special equipment, and there's no wrong way to do it. It's simply a matter of being present with yourself and allowing your mind to be calm amidst the chaos of daily life. So why not give it a try and see how meditation can benefit your life?

It's common for individuals to encounter spiritual struggles as they progress towards sobriety, but this is a natural part of the process. Our advice is to explore a variety of spiritual practices until you discover one that resonates with you.

By establishing a consistent spiritual practice, you will experience a range of benefits that include reducing the risk of relapse, improving your overall quality of life, and enhancing your journey towards sobriety. So, keep an open mind, explore different options, and find a practice that nourishes your soul and supports your journey.

❑

CHAPTER 7

555 Method

Looking for a powerful way to start your day and boost productivity? Look no further than the 555-morning mindfulness practice. With just 15 minutes of your time each morning, you can enhance your mental and spiritual well-being and set the tone for a productive day ahead.

This simple yet effective practice involves five minutes of meditation, five minutes of stretching, and five minutes of mentally preparing for the day. By taking a few moments to focus on your breath and observe your thoughts without judgement, you will cultivate a sense of inner peace and clarity that can carry you throughout the day.

Adding a few gentle stretches to your morning routine can help increase blood flow and flexibility, leaving you feeling refreshed and energised. And by mentally preparing for the day ahead, you will have a clear sense of your priorities and be ready to tackle whatever challenges come your way.

So why not try the 555-morning mindfulness practice for a week and see how it can transform your daily routine? After all, as the saying goes: 'The secret to a long life is to keep moving'.

369 Method

The 369 method is a manifestation technique that is believed to help individuals manifest their desires by focusing their thoughts and energy on what they want to achieve. It involves writing down your desires and intentions in a specific format and repeating them to yourself daily for a period.

The 369 method involves writing your desire three times in the morning, six times in the afternoon, and nine times at night for 21 days. The repetition is thought to help the subconscious mind align with your conscious thoughts and increase the likelihood of manifesting your desires.

Here is an example of how to use the 369 method:

Let's say your desire is to start a successful business. You would write down your intention in a specific format, such as: "I am grateful for my successful business that provides me with financial abundance and allows me to make a positive impact in the world."

Then, you would write this intention down three times in the morning, six times in the afternoon, and nine times at night for 21 consecutive days. You may choose to write it on a piece of paper, in a journal, or on a digital device. Just remember to write it word by word and not to simply copy and paste if working on a digital device.

As you repeat this affirmation to yourself, it is essential to focus on the feeling of already having achieved your desire and to believe in the possibility of it becoming a reality. You can also visualise your desired outcome and take steps towards your goal to increase your chances of manifestation.

Discover your gifts!

Often, we may hear the phrase 'If only you knew how great you are', but the truth is, it can be difficult to recognise our own greatness. Sometimes we may feel inadequate or lacking in certain areas, causing our self-confidence to dwindle. However, it is important to remember that as children of the Almighty, we all possess unique gifts and talents that are intended to help us fulfil our divine purpose. By recognising and utilising these gifts, we can strengthen our relationship with the Almighty and inspire others to do the same.

Do you ever feel like you are missing out on some hidden talents and gifts? Well, you are not alone! Many people struggle with recognising their own unique abilities. But do not worry, there are plenty of ways to discover these hidden treasures within yourself. Here are nine ideas to get you started:

1. **Ask others for their input:** Sometimes, it takes an outside perspective to see what we cannot.

   For example, you could ask a friend or family member what they think your strengths are or ask for feedback on a project you are working on to see if they notice any skills that you might be overlooking.

2. **Look for the silver lining in adversity:** Hard times can bring out the best in us, so focus on using your best qualities and gifts during tough times.

   Suppose you are going through a difficult time at work. Instead of dwelling on the negative aspects, focus on using your organisational or problem-solving skills to find creative solutions to the problems you are facing.

3. **Pray for guidance:** The Almighty knows our true potential and can help us recognise our gifts.

   You can try this:

   Dear God, I am feeling lost and unsure of my direction in life. I know that you have given me unique gifts and talents, but I am struggling to identify them. Please guide me and show me the path that I should take to use my gifts to serve you and others. Help me to recognise the signs and opportunities that you put in my path so that I can fulfil my true potential. Thank you for your love and guidance.

4. **Do not be afraid to step out of your comfort zone:** Trying new things can help you discover talents you never knew you had.

Let's say you have always been interested in music but never tried playing an instrument. Stepping out of your comfort zone and taking a music class or learning to play an instrument could help you discover hidden musical talents.

5. **Search for clues in the scriptures:** God often gives us hints about our gifts and how to develop them. If you are a believer, you could search the scriptures for stories about people who used their gifts for good and see what lessons you can learn from their experiences.

6. **Look for ways to serve others:** Our best qualities often shine when we are focused on helping those around us. Volunteering at a local charity or helping a friend in need can provide opportunities to use your best qualities and develop new skills.

7. **Think about your role models:** What gifts do they have that you also possess?

   If your role model is an athlete, you could try a new sport and see if you have similar skills. If your role model is a writer, you could try writing yourself and see if you have a natural talent for it.

8. **Reflect on your family:** What gifts do you share with your loved ones?

   Thinking about your family's strengths can help you see patterns in your own gifts. For example, if you come from a family of artists, you might have a natural inclination towards creativity as well.

9. **Study your patriarchal blessing:** A patriarchal blessing is a personal blessing given by a spiritual leader in some faiths. If you have one, you could reflect on the specific talents and abilities it mentions and consider how you can develop and use them in your life.

   An example of reflecting on a patriarchal blessing could be a person who received a blessing that mentions their musical abilities. They could reflect on their passion for music and consider how they can develop and use this gift to serve others and fulfil their potential. They may decide to take music lessons, join a choir, or volunteer to perform at local events. By using their talents in this way, they can live up to the potential mentioned in their blessing and make a positive impact on those around them.

Ways to strengthen your spirituality

Embarking on a spiritual journey is a unique experience that requires constant adaptation, evolution and growth. What may have worked for you at the beginning of your journey may not be suitable for your current state. Therefore, it's essential to develop a stronger bond with your higher power, true self, and others to strengthen your spiritual journey actively.

History has taught us that spiritual strength requires intentional and dedicated practices, often fuelled by enduring pain and suffering. Nevertheless, the path to spiritual growth is individualistic, and what works for you may not work for your loved ones.

Whether you are feeling stagnant, indifferent, or craving spiritual expansion, we've got you covered. Here are four practical ways to elevate your spiritual journey.

1. Practice forgiveness

Forgiveness is a mighty force that can spark a significant transformation in your life. In this world, we often face terrible situations, and it is likely that you've been severely hurt by someone in the past. Holding onto the hurt and resentment can only cause negativity to breed, ultimately hardening your heart. And you may not realise it, but that grudge is affecting you far more than the person who wronged you.

Although forgiveness is not an easy task, it is an essential step toward healing and genuine connection with your authentic self. Allow your higher power to strengthen you to forgive those who have hurt you. Surround yourself with supportive mentors, friends or spiritual guides who can help you navigate through the process.

If you are searching for inspiration, look to Mahatma Gandhi, a wise soul who said, "The weak can never forgive. Forgiveness is the attribute of the strong."

2. Stay open and honest with others!

Spirituality is a deeply personal journey, but it becomes more powerful when shared with others. It is tempting to present a polished version of ourselves to the world, but true authenticity comes from embracing our imperfections and being vulnerable with those we trust.

Opening and sharing our fears, doubts and mistakes with others can be daunting, but it can also be incredibly freeing. By being accepted for who we are, we can let go of the pressure to be perfect and embrace the messiness of life.

If you are ready to take the leap and share your true self with others, there are many ways to do so. Consider having a heart-to-heart with a trusted friend, joining a support group, talking to a spiritual leader, or seeking counselling or coaching from a professional who will listen with an open mind.

Remember, it is never too late to start living authentically and connecting with others in a meaningful way.

3. Explore your inner self!

Have you ever taken the time to truly get to know yourself? It may sound like a daunting task, but it is an essential step in creating a life that aligns with your values and purpose. By identifying what brings you joy and what drains your energy, you can make intentional choices that honour your unique way of being.

There are many ways to begin exploring your true self. You could start by journaling about times in your life when you felt fulfilled or unfulfilled, looking for patterns that can provide insight into what you need more or less of in your life now. Or you could speak to someone you can rely upon or trust to allow you to open up your heart and feelings without being judgemental about whatever you say. This process is extremely helpful in gaining awareness of what you need to achieve balance.

Another option is to meet with a spiritual leader who can guide you through self-exploration activities and practices. And of course, meditation is always a powerful tool for gaining clarity and insight into your true self.

4. Create a 'Rule of Life'

Your 'Rule of Life' is not just a set of guidelines, but a personalised roadmap for your spiritual journey, outlining the practices that you commit to regularly engaging in to maintain your connection to your higher power, true self and others. By establishing a framework of intentional practices, you can create a more fulfilling and meaningful life.

Creating a Rule of Life can be a transformative experience, but it can also be intimidating. Do not worry if you don't follow it exactly or if you need to adjust along the way. Remember to be gentle with yourself and stay flexible.

To cultivate your connection to a higher power, consider integrating practices such as prayer, meditation or moments of silence into your daily routine. For deeper self-awareness and connection to your true self, practices such as solitude, journaling and creative expression can be invaluable. To build meaningful connections with others, try attending spiritual gatherings, regularly scheduling dinners with friends and family, or participating in retreats.

It is important to keep in mind that your Rule of Life should be tailored to your unique needs and circumstances. Do not set yourself up for failure by establishing unrealistic goals. Start small and build gradually, incorporating practices that fit into your existing schedule and align with your interests.

Remember that your mind, body and spirit are interconnected, so taking care of yourself in all three realms is essential for a balanced life. If you are feeling exhausted or unwell, it may be difficult to effectively engage in spiritual practices. Prioritise self-care by getting enough rest and nourishing your body with healthy food and exercise.

By committing to a Rule of Life, you are embarking on a journey of self-discovery and personal growth. Embrace the process and enjoy the benefits of a more intentional, fulfilling and spiritually connected life.

5. Strengthen your mind, body and soul

Have you ever felt a mental or physical tension that left you feeling drained and disconnected? It is easy to get caught up in the daily grind and forget to check-in with us. However, taking a moment to pause and tune in can do wonders for our overall well-being.

The mind-body-soul connection may sound like a trendy concept, but it is backed by science. By taking care of our mental, physical and spiritual health, we can achieve greater balance and harmony in all areas of our lives.

Now, we will explore 13 practical steps to help you strengthen your mind-body-soul connection. From simple breathing exercises to self-reflection practices, you will discover how to tap into your inner wisdom and cultivate a more holistic approach to life. So, grab a cup of tea, find a comfortable spot, and let's dive in!

Are you feeling stuck in a rut? Do you want to strengthen your mind, body, and soul connection? Here are multiple ways to do it:

1. **Meditate**: Meditation has shown to reduce stress and increase mindfulness, helping you react calmly to stressful situations. There are many ways to meditate, from traditional sitting meditation to more active forms like dancing or drawing.
2. **Learn something new**: Learning a new skill or hobby helps keep your brain active and healthy, creating and strengthening new neural connections. Whether it is a

language or an instrument, never underestimate the power of learning.

3. **Get enough sleep**: Sleep is essential for your overall health, affecting everything from your mood to your metabolism. Lack of sleep in middle age is linked to a higher risk of Alzheimer's, so make sure you are getting between seven and nine hours of sleep per night.
4. **Find your passion**: Making time for the things you enjoy can help regulate your emotions and contribute to greater energy and vitality. Whether it is a hobby or a career change, finding your passion can greatly improve your well-being.
5. **Take time off in our society:** It is often seen as a badge of honour to work long hours and never take a break. However, rest and relaxation are crucial for your health. Block out time for rest in your schedule, prioritise spending time with loved ones, and avoid working during weekends and holidays. Remember, self-care is not selfish.
6. **Develop a growth mindset:** Having a growth mindset can help you bounce back from unexpected setbacks and see challenges as opportunities for personal growth.
7. **Get moving with exercise:** Exercise not only keeps your body healthy but also improves your mood, reduces

stress, and promotes brain health. Find activities you enjoy and make physical activity a part of your daily routine.

8. **Fuel your body with a balanced diet:** What you eat affects not only your physical health but also your thoughts, emotions and beliefs. Prioritise a diet rich in fruits and vegetables, limit your intake of meat, alcohol and sugar, and drink plenty of water.

9. **Practice yoga and breathwork:** Yoga can help release emotional tension stored in your body and calm your mind. Adding breathwork to your practice can enhance the benefits, such as stress reduction and increased energy.

10. **Cultivate gratitude:** Expressing gratitude regularly can improve your mood and overall well-being by shifting your focus to the positive aspects of your life.

11. **Connect with nature:** Spending time in nature has been shown to benefit your mind, body and soul. Aim for at least two hours a week in a natural setting to reap the rewards.

12. **Serve others:** Helping others is not only good for them but also for you. Find ways to give back, whether through a religious community, volunteering or activism.

13. **Practice self-compassion:** Being kind to yourself when facing failure or mistakes can help you develop greater

compassion for others and lead to a more loving and peaceful life.

By nurturing the connections among your mind, body and soul, you can unlock a path towards a happier, healthier and more vibrant version of yourself. This transformation can have a profound impact on how you feel and how you approach life, creating a ripple effect that touches every aspect of your existence.

❑

CHAPTER 8

Having a 'Pure Soul' ... What Does It Mean?

The term 'pure soul' can hold different meanings depending on the individual's perspective. A pure soul is characterised by honest intentions and an intrinsic motivation to do good, without seeking recognition or rewards. Another perspective suggests that a pure soul is someone who demonstrates compassion and selflessness towards others, treating everyone equally and being willing to make sacrifices for them.

From a religious or philosophical viewpoint, a soul is seen as the fundamental essence of a human being, giving them their unique identity and humanity. A pure soul, in this context, signifies an untarnished and uncorrupted sense of self, free from the negativity and turmoil present in the world. For instance, in Jainism, a pure soul is liberated from the impurities of karma, such as greed, anger and lust.

Given the current state of the world, individuals with a pure soul are a rare find, but that does not mean we cannot strive to become one.

How to know if you have a pure soul?

Here are the characteristics that can be used as a gauge to determine whether someone has a pure soul:

1. **Willingness to help others:** A pure soul distinguishes themselves by their readiness to help others without expecting anything in return, driven solely by the belief that it is the right thing to do.
2. **Fairness to all:** They treat everyone fairly, without any consideration of race, colour, wealth or social standing.
3. **Empathy:** Pure souls possess strong empathy, which allows them to understand people's perspectives and experiences.
4. **Giving without expectation:** They give without expecting anything in return, be it material things, time or affection.
5. **Strong sense of justice:** Witnessing an injustice upsets them, and they strive to correct it to the best of their abilities.
6. **Animal rescue:** A pure soul is often willing to rescue animals and provide them with a loving home. A pure

soul would protect animals and will not let anyone harm them.

7. **Seeing the good in people:** Despite the world's negative state, pure souls still see the good in people, regardless of their reputation or actions.
8. **Willingness to apologise:** A pure soul has no issue apologising for their mistakes and accepts responsibility for their actions, demonstrating courage and humility.

Next, what is KARMA?

Have you ever questioned what karma is and how it can impact your life? Karma is a multifaceted concept, particularly in Hinduism and Buddhism. It is often summarised by the phrases 'What goes around comes around' and 'What you sow is what you reap'.

In Hinduism, karma refers to the connection between a person's mental or physical actions and the outcomes that follow those actions. It also pertains to the consequences of a person's actions in their past and current lives, as well as the cause-and-effect chain in ethics.

In Buddhism, karma refers to the principle of causality. The result of an action, whether verbal, mental or physical, is determined not only by the act itself but also by the intention behind it.

Working and science behind KARMA

Karma emphasises the importance of intentional actions, whereby helping someone in need creates a positive impression that can lead to receiving help in return when required. Conversely, harmful actions lead to negative consequences, such as not receiving help when needed or being harmed.

To understand how karma works, consider planting oregano seeds, which will yield oregano and not some other plant. Similarly, acting with good intentions generates happiness, while acting with ill intentions creates problems.

While some people may doubt the effectiveness of karma, especially when they witness dishonest individuals gaining power or kind people facing hardships, many still believe that good deeds lead to positive outcomes. However, some people's belief in karma may lead them to sacrifice their goals and ambitions, causing them to fall behind in life due to their inability to set boundaries while helping others.

What are the types of karma?

Karma can take on individual or collective forms. Individual karma is created through a person's thoughts, words and actions, while collective karma is generated when groups of people act together.

Karma can be classified as good or bad

Good karma results from positive actions that bring happiness to others, while bad karma is the consequence of intentional harm inflicted on others.

Karma is believed to have multiple dimensions, with Sanchita and Prarabdha being the most prominent.

- **Sanchita Karma** refers to the accumulation of karma from past lives, which is stored as information in a universal warehouse. It is believed that people can gain knowledge about the nature of the universe by accessing this warehouse.
- **Prarabdha Karma**, on the other hand, refers to the karma that one is meant to experience in their current lifetime. This is believed to be limited to what one can handle, as being exposed to all karma memories from past lives could be overwhelming and potentially fatal.

Principles of karma

There are four main principles of karma:

1. **Even small actions can have significant consequences:** Something that may seem insignificant to you could make a huge difference in someone else's life. Conversely, even a small negative action can have long-lasting effects.

2. **Karma is non-transferable**: You are responsible for your own karmic experiences and cannot transfer them to someone else. Similarly, no one else can experience your karma for you or remove it for you.

3. **Half-hearted actions won't bring the desired results:** To achieve the results you want, you must fully commit to your actions or intentions.

4. **Karmic actions do not disappear on their own:** You must experience the consequences, whether good or bad, or purify them through spiritual practices.

How does karma affect your life?

According to Buddhist philosophy, there is no divine being who rewards or punishes individuals for their actions. Instead, people are responsible for their own actions and the consequences that follow based on their intentions. Accidental occurrences do not count towards karmic justice or consequences. While there is no way to prove the existence of karma, believing in it can lead to stronger friendships and happiness, as people tend to do good to receive good in return.

Even if you do not believe in karma, treating others poorly can result in negative feelings and resentment, leading to unhappiness and problems in life. Therefore, many people believe in treating others the way they want to be treated, attributing it to the concept of karma.

Karma can influence how individuals lead their lives. Some may live in fear of the consequences of their actions, while others may anticipate future rewards.

How does karma affect your life?

Karma has an impact on your life in every aspect unless you are an enlightened being at a highly evolved level. Your life is essentially a continuous manifestation of karma.

The karmic software

Karma refers to action and is like energy that generates an equal and opposite reaction. It is not inherently good or bad but depends on how people perceive it. The result of an action must be obtained, and one cannot escape the consequences of their actions.

Actions create memories that lead to desires, and desires prompt further actions. For instance, taking a yoga class leads to a memory of the experience, and if enjoyable, a desire to attend more classes. These memories and desires create a karmic software that shapes one's life.

The energy produced by actions is stored in memories and desires and can manifest at any time. For example, you may forget about your yoga class but remember it months later while passing a yoga studio, leading to a desire to take another class.

What is the Vedantic view?

Belief in reincarnation is not a requirement for understanding karma, but the Vedantic perspective suggests that your current life is the result of actions performed over many previous lives. This belief can help explain why bad things happen to good people and why some innocent children develop life-threatening illnesses. Karma suggests that every situation in your life and everyone you meet has a karmic significance, and everything happens for a reason.

Karma implies that you are responsible for creating your own life. While free will exists, many people are trapped in cycles of habit and conditioning, repeating the same behaviour and wondering why their lives aren't improving. As you evolve spiritually, you can break out of these cycles and consciously choose the life you want to lead. The spiritual path involves releasing karma and memories that cloud your awareness and prevent you from remembering who you truly are. This process does not mean losing your memories and desires but rather detaching from them and freeing yourself from their influence. As Adi Shankara said, "I use memories, but I don't allow them to use me."

Gathering and storing karma

Your karma is not only the result of your own actions, but also influenced by factors such as your family, religion, race and nationality. Every situation you encounter in life is linked to karma. You continuously generate karma through your thoughts, words, actions, attitudes, expectations and lifestyle, whether consciously or unconsciously. Taking on someone else's karma, however, is generally not advisable, as it can be detrimental to your own growth. This can happen through stealing, gossiping or fantasising. In intimate relationships, taking on each other's karma can be a bonding experience, if the relationship is founded on love and enlightenment.

According to the Vedas, your karma is stored in the Jiva, or the individual soul, which is conditioned by karma. There are three types of karma: the one you chose to work through in this life, the one stored for future births, and the new karma you create in every moment. Chakras, or the subtle energy centres in your body, store the karma for this lifetime. Karma can distort your consciousness and create an illusory world. Clearing your karma can help you step out of this illusion and experience a higher reality.

Releasing your karma

Karma is inevitable and its energy is usually returned with the same intensity that generated it, resulting in either happiness or suffering based on past actions. However, every situation is an opportunity for growth and releasing karma, and could be considered as a positive outcome. Rather than being stuck in a cycle of paying for past mistakes, it is possible to transform, transmute or transcend karma through the quality of current actions. To achieve this, there are eight practices that can help improve the quality of your actions.

Here are eight practices that can help you increase the quality of your actions and transform your karma:

1. Be mindful of your choices and make quality choices. This can lessen the intensity or magnitude of situations resulting from returning karma. Also, your choices determine the quality of new karma being created and stored for future events.

2. Forgive those who have harmed you, even if you **cannot** forgive the act. Understanding that every hurt you encounter is the return of some karma can help you forgive and move forward.

3. Cultivate gratitude for everything in your life, as releasing karma is cause for celebration.

4. Look for growth opportunities in challenging situations instead of seeing them as problems. This allows you to release the karma and move ahead on your spiritual journey.

5. Learn from astrology by understanding your karmic probabilities. A competent astrologer can interpret your chart and give you advice.
6. Seek an enlightened teacher who can see your karmic patterns and advise you accordingly.
7. Discover your Dharma, your true purpose in life. Living in alignment with your Dharma means that your actions will become spontaneously correct, and you will never create karma.
8. Meditate, especially using mantras, which have no karma as they hold no memory or desire. With regular practice, meditation can realign you with your true self, lead you back to your Dharma, and allow you to wash away ill effects of bad karma on all levels. Commitment to your spiritual path is the key to escaping from the karmic prison and enjoying unbounded freedom in every moment.

How can you attract good karma?

The concept of karma is an age-old theory that suggests that our thoughts and actions dictate what we deserve in life. While some people believe that we can generate good karma by following a few simple rules, it is important to note that the benefits of doing so extend beyond just ourselves. By practicing these steps daily, we can bring positive karma into our lives and also contribute to the betterment of those around us.

Step 1 encourages us to focus on loving and forgiving ourselves. Many of us struggle with feelings of low self-esteem, self-blame, and self-doubt at some point in our lives. Instead of dwelling on the 'what ifs' and 'should haves' of our past, we can try to shift our attention to the positive aspects of our lives. Beginning each day with a daily affirmation can help us focus on self-love and the goodness in our lives. As our thinking changes, so too do our thoughts and actions towards those around us.

Step 2 emphasises the importance of loving and forgiving others. Holding grudges can hold us back in life. Although it is not always easy to forgive someone who has hurt us, it is better for both ourselves and the other person in the long run. By releasing ill feelings, we clear away negativity that can block good karma from manifesting in our lives.

Step 3 encourages us to practice kindness and compassion, which is one of the easiest ways to send positive karma into the world. As Gandhi ji once said, "Be the change you want to see in the world." In other words, if we desire to draw good karma into our lives, we must first practice what we hope to receive. The Golden Rule, which is a lesson taught in many cultures worldwide, reminds us to treat others as we would like to be treated ourselves.

Step 4 suggests that we spend time reflecting in quiet introspection in order to get good karma flowing into our lives. By exploring our personal role in all that has transpired in our lives without judgement, we can gain understanding and insight into how our thoughts and actions have contributed to our current situation.

Finally, **Step 5** emphasises the importance of consistency in practicing kindness, compassion, self-love, and responsibility for our words and actions. While change cannot happen overnight, as we continue to send positive karma out into the world, we begin to attract and receive good karma until it becomes a natural part of our daily life experience.

Seven master strategies to get rid of bad karma

1. Begin by identifying the areas of your life that feel stagnant and are preventing you from advancing towards your true potential. Reflect on when and how these issues started to get to the root of the problem.
2. Cut ties with toxic people who bring you more harm than good. Politely and respectfully distance yourself from such individuals to preserve your karma and set healthy boundaries.

3. Take responsibility for your mistakes, learn from them, and try to do things differently in the future. This will shift your energy and help you make better decisions in the long run.
4. Engage in activities that nourish your spirit and promote well-being. This includes eating healthy, exercising regularly, getting enough rest, and spending time in self-reflection.
5. Don't let your weaknesses define you. Instead, develop the courage to overcome them and take control of your karmic patterns.
6. Evaluate your old ways of doing things and modify your behaviour if they no longer serve you. Act with principle and do good, even when it is not expected of you.
7. Forgive everyone, including yourself. Resentment feeds bad karma and keeps you trapped in negative cycles. By letting go of anger and bitterness, you can detach from negative emotions and experience the liberation to fulfil your greater purpose.

❑

CHAPTER 9

All about Spiritual Awakening

What is a spiritual awakening?

Have you ever felt like you were going through multiple events without really being present in your own life? This is what it means to be living on autopilot. However, a spiritual awakening can jolt you out of this state and completely shift your perspective on life. It is the feeling of being in control of your own path and realising that there is more to life than what you have been experiencing. A spiritual awakening can happen gradually, with a gentle nudge to change your life, or it can happen suddenly, feeling like a jolt out of a dream-like state. If you experience the latter, you may feel an intense demand to change your life all at once. So, are you ready to awaken to a new reality?

What causes a spiritual awakening?

Have you ever felt like you were stuck in a rut and needed a change, but did not know where to start? According to spiritual teacher Christine Agro, a spiritual awakening can be the solution and I also strongly agree to this. However, it is important to note that you cannot force a spiritual awakening to happen. In fact, if you are already trying to awaken, you are already on the journey.

I also believe that there is always something that gets you to the point of awakening and usually it refers to the situation where we feel lost or broken and are looking for a breakthrough. It could be a toxic relationship, unfulfilling work, desire to conceive a child, unable to do well in studies—it would be different for everyone but the purpose would remain the same for all—Spiritual Awakening! These experiences can serve as a wake-up call, leading you to a new perspective on life. So, if you are feeling stuck and seeking a change, remember that a spiritual awakening can happen naturally, but it is up to you to be open and receptive to it. Who knows where this journey could take you?

Benefits of spiritual awakening

Embarking on a spiritual awakening journey opens a world of possibilities, according to experts. It is like discovering hidden rooms in a house you thought you knew inside out where you will learn more about yourself and how to live. An awakened state can make life easier, not by erasing challenges, but by changing the way you view them.

Gabbard's experience is also a testament to this. Her spiritual awakening helped her overcome addiction, and through clarity of thought, she was able to help others too. This journey can bring about relief, joy, grace and wisdom. You may develop a deeper understanding of yourself and your place in the world, which can lead to acceptance and even more blessings. A spiritual awakening is a gift that keeps on giving.

Are you going through a spiritual awakening? How to know?

The path to spiritual awakening can take many forms, and it is a unique experience for everyone. However, certain signs can indicate that you are undergoing a spiritual awakening. Keep an eye out for these informative signs, as they might provide valuable insight into your spiritual journey.

1. Breaking the cycle of patterns: Have you been stuck in the same cycle for a while without understanding why? When you finally realise your patterns, you might be going through a spiritual awakening.
2. Increased empathy: People who have gone through spiritual awakenings report feeling more empathetic and caring deeply about others.
3. Contentment with the things that once bothered you: Joy replaces discomfort as you become more aware of

energy around you and differentiate between your own feelings and others.

4. Heightened intuition and senses: Your intuition becomes stronger and more prominent, and you will experience the world more deeply through your senses.

5. Abandoning negativity and gossip: As you become more positive, you will let go of negative talk and gossip.

6. Living in the present moment: Instead of dwelling on the past or worrying about the future, you will learn to live in the present moment and embrace 'it is what it is' mentality.

7. Pursuing your goals: As your spiritual journey unfolds, you will feel a sense of responsibility and be inspired to pursue your goals and take on challenges that once seemed impossible.

8. Using your heart: You will spread love through random acts of kindness, social activism, and creative pursuits like writing or photography.

9. Harnessing your energy: Positive energy will become your greatest asset, and you will redirect your thoughts to create healing and transformation.

10. Letting go of attachments: Whether it's an ex or the need for validation from others, you will learn to let go of attachments that hold you back.

11. Affirming your desires: By affirming what you want to the universe, you will create space for your desires to manifest in unexpected ways.
12. Overcoming trauma: Your spiritual awakening will help you transform from past trauma and gain a better understanding of the world as a spiritual being.
13. Embracing authenticity: You will shed your masks and be your true self with no apologies or reservations.
14. Accepting death: Fear of death will no longer hold you back as you live life to the fullest and embrace your true self.
15. Finding inner peace: As your spiritual journey progresses, you will feel a sense of lightness and inner peace that radiates outward to those around you.

Are You Self-Awakened?

Self-awakening can lead to powerful transformations in our lives, but what sets self-awakened people apart from others? Here, we will explore the five empowering qualities of self-awakened individuals. From their drive for self-improvement to cultivating gratitude, seeking mentors, practicing spirituality, and building healthy relationships, these qualities can help guide you on your journey toward self-empowerment. So, if you are ready to challenge unhealthy habits and explore new experiences, read on to discover how you can begin your own journey of self-awakening. Remember, the power to change your life is within you.

Here are the five empowering qualities of self-awakened people:

Becoming self-awakened can be a powerful transformation, but how do some people manage to thrive despite obstacles while others do not? Here are some key traits of the self-awakened:

1. A drive for self-improvement: Rather than focusing on material goods, self-awakened individuals seek growth and challenge themselves. They are curious about their inner lives and eager to understand their powerful emotions.

2. A cultivated sense of gratitude: Self-awakened people find ways to appreciate life even in difficult circumstances. This can require effort, but the rewards are plentiful. By cultivating gratitude, they can shift the culture around them and inspire positivity in others.

3. A yearning for mentors: The self-awakened seek guidance from mentors who can provide encouragement and approval. They create reliable selves by absorbing the skill and expertise of their mentor.

4. A spiritual practice: A spiritual practice helps you move beyond the mundane and consider the profound, inspiring you to embrace a more altruistic way of being. By contemplating life's sufferings, you can re-evaluate your life choices and let go of petty concerns.
5. Healthy relationships: Negative relationships can cause great suffering. The self-awakened identify unhealthy relationships and move toward positive people to strive toward a more fulfilling life.

To begin your journey of self-awakening, challenge unhealthy habits, and explore new experiences. Seek inspiration from healing and wellness sessions, support groups, classes, meditation and other creative outlets. Remember, self-awakening begins with you. By taking full responsibility for your choices, you can take a significant step toward self-empowerment and a new way of being.

Am I Having Spiritual Awakening?

Spirituality is a concept that can be interpreted in various ways depending on who you ask. At its core, it involves a recognition of something beyond our individual selves, something bigger and more profound. It is like sensing that there's a hidden layer to our existence, beyond what we can see, hear, touch or taste. This could mean feeling connected to a larger, more cosmic force or believing in a higher power that guides us.

What sets spirituality apart from religion is that it is often a personal pursuit rather than a shared belief system. Unlike religion, which can have a set of prescribed practices and rituals, spirituality is more about finding one's own purpose and inner peace. So, whether you are drawn to meditation, nature, art, or any other form of self-exploration, spirituality can be a deeply enriching journey that is uniquely your own.

What is a spiritual awakening?

A spiritual awakening is like hitting the reset button on your mind, causing a profound shift in your perception of the world around you. It can be a transformative experience, leading to a heightened state of consciousness and a newfound sense of purpose. People describe it using different words like enlightenment, bliss, or even discovering nirvana. This awakening can be both daunting and exhilarating at the same time, like a rollercoaster ride for your soul. Interestingly, the concept of spiritual awakening in the Western world was first introduced by the famed psychiatrist Carl Jung, who viewed it as a journey of rediscovering one's true self.

What triggers a spiritual awakening?

A spiritual awakening can be sparked by a multitude of life experiences, from the highs of triumphs to the lows of traumatic events. It can also occur gradually without any clear trigger, through practices that promote greater self-awareness, like mindfulness, meditation, or connecting with nature.

But how can you tell if you are experiencing a spiritual awakening? Are there any signs or symptoms to look out for?

Signs of spiritual awakening

Here are some possible rephrased points that highlight the intriguing aspects of a spiritual awakening:

- You may experience an increased sense of intuition, enabling you to detect when someone is being inauthentic or manipulative.
- Your dreams may become more vivid, offering insights into your subconscious thoughts and desires.
- You might feel drawn to spend more time in nature, meditate, or practice mindfulness, even if it means changing your habits or routine.
- You may feel a stronger connection to the world around you, whether it's through a deeper appreciation of nature or a heightened sense of empathy.
- You may feel the need to re-evaluate your beliefs or priorities, which could lead to significant changes in your life, such as pursuing a different career or giving back to your community.

- You might experience synchronicities, where seemingly unrelated events or experiences are connected in meaningful ways.
- You may feel more alone or disconnected from people and activities that used to bring you joy.
- You might feel a desire to give back or be of service to others, whether it's through volunteering, supporting environmental causes, or helping those in need.
- You may experience physical symptoms like fatigue or heightened sensory awareness as your body adjusts to the changes in your mental and emotional state.

Goal of spiritual awakening

A spiritual awakening can bring about a whole new level of understanding and perspective in your life. It can fill you with a sense of profound joy, wisdom, grace and relief, making you feel like you have finally discovered your true self and your place in the world. As your awareness deepens, you may find yourself feeling more at peace with life's challenges, and even manifesting positivity in all aspects of your life. So, get ready to embrace a new level of consciousness and unlock the mysteries of the universe with a spiritual awakening!

How can one have spiritual awakening?

Spiritual awakenings can occur unexpectedly and at any point in life but can also be influenced by intentional practices such as meditation, mindfulness and self-care. While decluttering your life and expanding your knowledge can help set you on the path to spirituality, it's important to remember that awakening cannot be forced. Instead, it requires openness and a willingness to examine your beliefs and embrace the possibility of something greater.

Can other people help you in becoming more spiritual?

Have you ever felt like there is something more to life than what you see? Something deeper, more profound and purposeful? This is where spirituality comes in. It is about discovering your unique purpose and living a life aligned with it. But sometimes, this journey can be challenging and overwhelming. This is where a mentor, teacher or spiritual coach can be invaluable. They can help you, guide you, provide support, and keep you accountable as you navigate the twists and turns of your spiritual journey. With their help, you can unlock your full potential and experience true happiness and fulfilment.

What is spiritual coaching?

If you feel like you are struggling to find your purpose or direction in life, working with a spiritual coach could be just what you need. They can offer support and guidance to help you create a plan for achieving your goals and hold you accountable as you journey towards self-discovery.

Spirituality coaching takes many different approaches, ranging from holistic to religious. Regardless of the approach, the main focus is on your present situation and how you can create a brighter future. However, if you are struggling with past experiences and how they are impacting your present, a counsellor may be a better fit for your needs.

Ways to Connect with Your Higher Self

1. Set the stage: Prepare your meditation space with items that bring you joy, calmness and positive energy. Even good food can contribute to your meditation rituals and infuse loving and healing energy into your body. The food you eat can greatly impact your energy levels, so be mindful of high-frequency foods.
2. Watch your breath: Take deep cleansing breaths, feel your body from head to toe, and scan how each area feels in the present moment. Inhale your dreams and desires and exhale the negative energy that takes away from them.
3. Watch your thoughts: Allow all thoughts to flow without judging or labelling them. If bombarded with thoughts, take a break and walk around before meditating again. Consider thoughts as data rather than attaching feelings or meaning to them.

4. Be gentle with yourself: Allow the energy you draw to serve you. If it doesn't, let it go without blame or judgement. Clearing your mind through meditation creates the foundation for manifesting intentions in the present moment.
5. Affirm what you want: Write a list of manifestations you wish to attract, in the present tense, and attach the feeling of how you want to feel when they become a reality. Focus on how your future self will feel when you manifest your goals.
6. Let your manifestations go: Once you have stated your intentions and attached feelings, let them go. Trust that the universe will incubate your manifestations in the ether.
7. Reflect on your manifestations: Revisit your list from time to time and celebrate your progress. You may seal your list in an envelope and address it to yourself, requesting someone to send it to you at a time when it resonates with you the most.
8. Celebrate your wins: Take time to show gratitude and recognition for your wins, big or small. Write them down and savour them as a reminder of your achievements.

Ways to Harness Your Inner Power

Building inner power is crucial for achieving success and happiness in life. It is about cultivating a strong sense of self-worth and resilience that helps you overcome obstacles and challenges. Here are eight ways to build your inner power:

1. Own your stories: Embrace your failures and share your stories of how you overcame them. By acknowledging your struggles and victories, you remind yourself of your strength and power. Your experiences make you unique and resilient, and they can inspire others too.
2. Do something that scares you: Challenging yourself to do something that you have been afraid of can break the cycle of feeling powerless. It can remind you that you are brave and capable of handling new challenges. Stepping out of your comfort zone can also help you grow and learn new skills.
3. Use powerful body language: Your body language can influence your thoughts and emotions. When you stand in a confident position, your body tells your brain that you can handle anything. Relax your shoulders, widen your stance, uncross your arms, hold your head high, and make eye contact with a smile. This can help you feel more confident and powerful.
4. Know your superpowers: It is important to focus on your strengths and what you are really good at. Stop trying to be good at everything and instead, focus on your unique talents and skills. By leveraging your strengths, you can achieve more and feel more confident.

5. Spend time with people with positive vibes: Surround yourself with people who inspire and motivate you. Spend time with those who believe in you, make you feel good, and celebrate your journey. Positive energy is contagious, and being around uplifting people can help you feel more powerful and confident.
6. Spend time alone in silence: Take time to reflect on your inner voice and get to know yourself better. Create quietness for your inner voice to be heard. This can help you gain clarity and insight into your thoughts and emotions and make better decisions.
7. Start your day in control: Creating healthy habits that are as automatic as brushing your teeth can help you feel more in control of your day. Daily reflection and mindset work can help you build a strong framework for your day and create a positive outlook.
8. Take care of your body and space: Cultivate a healthy body and a positive living environment. Drink water, take a shower, put on clean clothes, and move your body. Cultivate a home that you feel good in and carve out a space where you feel calm and amazing. If you cannot relax in your body and space, you start every day at a deficit. By taking care of your physical and emotional needs, you can feel more powerful and in control of your life.

Ways to Start A Spiritual Conversation

Engaging in spiritual conversations and sharing the good insights with others is an essential part of living spiritually. However, for many, it can be a daunting task. Fear, doubt and uncertainty can hold us back from taking the first step. But with a few practical tips and a willingness to step out of our comfort zones, we can have meaningful conversations that leave a lasting impact.

The first tip is to take the first step.

Starting a conversation is the foundation for any meaningful dialogue. But, more often than not, we miss or avoid opportunities to engage in spiritual conversations because we are unsure of where to start. Overcoming our fears and doubts by praying and taking that initial step can lead to life-changing conversations.

Ask questions

Asking questions is another great way to start a conversation and transition into spiritual topics. By showing a genuine interest in the other person, we can create a connection that builds trust and understanding. Asking about their life, family, or opinions on a topic can help us find common ground, which can lead to deeper discussions about faith and spirituality.

Active listening

Active listening is key to establishing a connection with others. When we listen intently to what they are saying, we can learn more about their beliefs and experiences. We can also find common ground and keywords that will help guide the conversation towards spiritual topics. When we show others that we are truly interested in what they have to say, they are more likely to open up to us.

Find common ground

Finding common ground is another important aspect of having meaningful conversations. We can discover shared experiences, interests or concerns that can help create a comfortable space to talk about spiritual matters. If they are going through a difficult time, we can offer comfort and hope by sharing how our faith helped us through a similar experience.

Gently shift the conversation

Once we have established a rapport and found common ground, we can gently shift the conversation towards spiritual topics. Asking what they believe about God (Supreme Power) or if they have a faith can lead to a deeper discussion about the subject. Sharing our own beliefs and experiences can also help create a non-threatening and relevant environment for others to explore their spirituality.

Reconnect

Finally, it is important to connect with others beyond the initial conversation. Leaving our contact information or getting theirs allows us to follow up and continue the conversation. We can continue to encourage and support them on their spiritual journey, even if it is just by checking in from time to time.

Remember, making disciples is a journey, not a destination. By intentionally starting conversations and connecting with others spiritually, you can make a meaningful impact on their spiritual journey. So, be bold, be intentional, and trust in your higher self to guide you every step of the way.

Spiritual Development: The Seven Stages

Did you know that you are more than just a physical body? You have a spiritual side waiting to be fully embraced! The journey to exploring your spirituality is a personal choice, and along the way, you will encounter opportunities for growth and development. At first, most people follow a similar path, but at certain points, you will be faced with a decision: continue on the same mundane path or delve into the wonders of your spiritual journey. These moments can happen at any time, so it is essential to pay attention to your heart's intuition and be open to new possibilities. Are you ready to embark on an exciting spiritual adventure?

1. Innocence

From the moment you enter this material world, you are swept up in the hustle and bustle of daily life, driven by the desires that this material world brings along. But in your early days, basking in the warmth of your family's love and care, you are still intimately connected to the divine and the infinite expanse of consciousness you just emerged from. Yet, as you grow up, the world begins to teach you how to conform, and slowly but surely, the memory of your spiritual origin starts to fade. It is a rare few who are able to hold onto their divine connection and walk the path of spiritual greatness.

2. Ego and fear

As you mature, your ego comes to the forefront, and suddenly you realise that your fate is entirely dependent on the people around you. The unadulterated love that once enveloped you is gradually overtaken by fear and its accompanying emotions. You come to the realisation that in order to achieve your desires, you must cater to those in authority. As you develop your character, you start weaving the tales that will ultimately mould and distinguish your existence.

3. Power

In the pursuit of conquering fear, you pave the way for triumph in your life. You receive education, establish a career and family, all in the hopes of obtaining control and eliminating fear. You amass material possessions as a means of feeling secure.

Now, for some, this is where their journey ends. They become fixated on acquiring more power and control, continuously seeking to satiate their material desires. These individuals remain at stage 3, perpetually centred on themselves.

However, for others, a realisation dawns upon them—there must be more to life than just the accumulation of possessions and power. They begin to search for a deeper meaning to existence and awaken spiritually, embarking on stage 4 of their journey.

4. Giving

As you enter this stage, you start to recognise that life is not merely about attaining personal power and accumulating material possessions. You begin to inquire about ways in which you can contribute to society and serve the world. You develop a sense of ease with both giving and receiving.

Nevertheless, it is important to note that giving can also lead to a sense of control. At this phase, giving may still be driven by ego, where you expect something in return or derive a sense of satisfaction from it.

The first option is to continue giving from the standpoint of the ego, where you do many admirable things in the world. However, this may impede your complete spiritual growth.

The second option presents itself when you start to give from a place of love and empathy without any anticipation of recognition or reward. Your giving becomes selfless, and your authentic spiritual journey commences.

5. The seeker

At this juncture, you initiate your customary spiritual routines, and the yearning for enlightenment intensifies within you. Most of your choices are now governed by the fourth chakra, the centre of the heart.

You embark on a quest to discover the profound significance of things. You endeavour to comprehend the purpose of your existence and how to infuse more meaning into your life. You may seek the guidance of teachers and masters, read books, and adopt various techniques. You catch glimpses of the ultimate objective that motivate you to remain on the path.

As you progress, your throat chakra begins to expand, enabling you to articulate the qualities of the heart in your daily life.

6. The sage

At this point, Cosmic Consciousness arises, and your mind is fully awakened. You become a mere observer of your actions and realise that you are merely playing various roles in life. The fear of death dissolves as you comprehend that life is just another role to play. You gain access to basic yogic powers, yet there is still a distinction between the giver and the receiver.

However, another pivotal moment in your spiritual journey is approaching. At this stage, the ego still lingers, and the error you can make is to believe that you are unique. You might wrongly believe that you have achieved the ultimate goal and advertise yourself as such. The end is within reach, but the ego obscures it from view, keeping you imprisoned in a false sense of spiritual accomplishment.

The alternative decision is to acknowledge the presence of the ego but not allow it to control you. You can permit it to find its place in the bigger picture peacefully. You persist in your expedition with modesty and devotion, and you give solely for the sake of giving. Your perspective shifts from 'What's in it for me' to 'How can I serve?'

As you progress, spiritual insights and inspiration flourish, and you start to hear the voice of the inner guru as the sixth chakra unlocks.

7. Spirit

In the seventh and final stage, the yogi experiences a complete awakening of the heart, and divine and Unity Consciousness are fully realised. The concept of separation dissolves, and the yogi perceives the interconnectedness of all things in the universe. Spiritual practice becomes pure joy, as all chakras are open and spiritual energy flows freely.

At this point, there is no longer any need for decision-making. The yogi lives in perfect harmony with nature, and everything needed is provided at exactly the right moment. The yogi becomes the embodiment of the Totality.

While the material world may seem enticing at first, the yogi comes to understand that the spiritual path leads to the experience of the true self and eternal bliss. Material possessions and pursuits are seen as fleeting and ultimately unfulfilling.

The great yogi feels that by not following a spiritual path, eternal bliss has been renounced for the sake of a few passing moments of happiness. The material world is like a dry garden, waiting for the knowledge of the divine to make it bloom. In contrast, the spiritual path leads to unbounded freedom and tapping into Cosmic Energy.

Each moment becomes a spiritual act when done with awareness, and the yogi finds inner peace through regular and disciplined spiritual practice. Even if the path is occasionally lost, the spiritual journey ultimately becomes a way of life, a lush oasis in the desert of mundane existence. The ego will always try to limit and control, but with wise choices and perseverance, the true self can be realised.

❑

CHAPTER 10

Surrendering yourself to Spirituality

Have you ever considered that 'surrender' could be the key to achieving infinite freedom and endless possibilities in your spiritual journey? You might associate surrender with weakness or defeat, but it is the most powerful action you can take. Surrender means putting your trust in a higher power, whether it is God, the universe, or some other divine force, to guide you through life's ups and downs.

At the spiritual level, everything is always unfolding perfectly, without the need for struggle or force. It is only our ego-mind that convinces us we are isolated individuals fighting to survive in a hostile world. But the truth is that we are spiritual beings, and when we surrender to the higher power, we open ourselves up to a world of possibilities. By letting go of fear and doubt, we remove the obstacles that our ego has created.

Of course, letting go all at once is not possible—it's a process of many small steps that involves replacing automatic reactions with a deeper awareness. But by following these simple guidelines, you can start down the path of surrender and discover the freedom and peace that come with it.

1. Know about your intentions

Your soul's path is fuelled by intention, and every day you have the power to bring yourself closer to it by letting go of the false desires that stem from your ego. Don't let fear, greed or anger control your intentions. Instead, stay aware of the feeling-tone they carry and refuse to buy into them. By unmasking your false intentions, you will be able to close the gap between your true destiny and the delusions of your ego. So, keep your eyes open, your mind clear, and your heart pure as you navigate the twists and turns of your soul's journey.

2. Set your intentions high

Why not strive to be a saint and a miracle worker? After all, the ultimate goal of inner growth is mastery. So, why not ask for it and start acquiring it right away? Don't stress yourself out by trying to perform extraordinary feats, but don't deny yourself the possibility of achieving them either. It all starts with vision—train yourself to see the everyday miracles around you, and you'll find it easier to cultivate even greater ones. With dedication and a willingness to see the extraordinary in the ordinary, you too can become a true master of the miraculous.

3. See yourself in the new light

The ego has a sneaky way of making you feel like you are lacking in power and constantly in need. This creates a voracious appetite to accumulate everything you can get your hands on—money, status, sex, pleasure—in an attempt to fill the void. But the harsh truth is that these things will never be enough. Luckily, you can break free from this cycle of emptiness by seeing yourself in a new light. Believe it or not, you and a saint are not so different—the only distinction is the size of your light. Both of you are shining beacons of light in this world, and realising this truth can be the key to your liberation from the grip of ego.

4. See everyone in the light

Despite our differences, we all bask in the same radiant light of existence. So, before you are quick to judge someone else—no matter how much you think they deserve it—take a moment to remember that every single person is trying their best from their own unique perspective. After all, we are all operating from our own level of consciousness. So, instead of jumping to conclusions or harshly criticising others, try to see them with a more compassionate and understanding eye. By doing so, you will not only elevate the collective consciousness but also cultivate a deeper sense of empathy and kindness within yourself.

5. Remind yourself everyday what truly matters

Life can often feel like a never-ending whirlwind of chaos, with the ego constantly clamouring for attention. But do not let that distract you from your spiritual purpose. It is crucial to remind yourself every single day of what truly matters. For some, jotting down their intentions on paper can be helpful, while others may find solace in consistent meditation or prayer. Whatever your method may be, it is important to find your centre and take a close look at yourself. Hold onto your intentions tightly until they become rooted deep within you. When you are able to maintain a steadfast focus on your spiritual path, you will find that the chaos of everyday life begins to fade away, replaced by a sense of inner calm and purpose.

6. Forgive yourself

It is all too easy to fall into the traps of selfishness and deception, even when we least expect it. We have all experienced that sudden pang of guilt after making a hurtful remark or succumbing to the temptation to cheat. But here is the thing—it is okay to forgive yourself for these slip-ups. Just as you would show understanding and empathy towards others, it is important to extend that same kindness to yourself. Remember that you are doing the best you can from your own level of awareness. In fact, some of the most enlightened individuals are those who constantly stumble but never give up. So, if you find yourself in a moment of weakness, dust yourself off and keep moving forward with compassion and resilience.

7. Learn the art of letting go

Being spiritual is a paradoxical journey—one where you can be both right and wrong simultaneously. On one hand, you are absolutely right for seeking a deeper connection with the divine. But on the other hand, you are wrong to assume that things will remain the same forever. The truth is, every step of your spiritual evolution is necessary and divinely orchestrated, but there comes a point when you must release your grip and move forward. It can be tempting to cling to what is familiar, but true growth requires a willingness to let go of what no longer serves you. Remember, the path to spiritual enlightenment is an ever-changing journey. So, embrace the paradox and trust in the unfolding of your higher purpose.

8. Revere what is holy

Today, it is easy to become sceptical of anything related to spirituality or the divine. Maybe you were not raised with a strong religious background, or perhaps you have simply never taken the time to explore the world's sacred texts. But here is the thing—the writings of saints and spiritual leaders are a limitless source of wisdom and inspiration, just waiting to be discovered. They have the power to awaken your heart and nourish your soul, providing the perfect catalyst for growth and transformation. So, do not be afraid to dip into this vast treasure trove of knowledge. Who knows, you may just stumble upon the exact words you need to help your soul bloom and flourish.

9. Allow your spirit to lead

Do you often find yourself worrying, trying to control everything, and constantly doubting yourself? Well, you are not alone. Many people struggle with these addictive tendencies, which can lead to stress, anxiety and a general sense of dissatisfaction with life. But what if there was a better way? What if you could let go of the need to micromanage everything and instead allow the universe to guide you towards your true purpose? It may sound scary, but it is worth a try. Trust that everything will work out as it should and be open to new opportunities that come your way. Who knows, the outcome you have been struggling to force may not be the best one for you after all. So why not take a step back and let your spirit take the wheel for a change?

10. Embrace the unknown

You are not just the sum of your experiences and preferences; there is a deeper, truer version of yourself waiting to be revealed. But you cannot force this true self to come out all at once. It takes time and patience to peel away the layers of illusion and allow your soul to emerge.

When you embrace the unknown and allow yourself to follow new impulses and uplifting thoughts, you tap into a part of yourself that is beyond the limitations of your past. This is where God resides, and when you fully embrace the unknown, you unlock the door to true freedom. So, cherish these moments of discovery, like a newborn baby, and trust that the unknown is leading you towards a more authentic, fulfilling life.

As we come to the end of this book, let me leave you here with these thoughts. Spirituality is a journey that is unique to everyone, and it requires a willingness to explore and question our beliefs, thoughts, and emotions. Remember that spirituality is not limited to any particular religion or belief system, but rather it is a way of connecting with the deeper aspects of ourselves and the world around us. Take the time to reflect on what you have learned and continue to cultivate the qualities of self-awakened individuals in your life. May the wisdom and insights gained from this book help you on your spiritual journey, and may spirituality continue to connect with you in meaningful ways.

❑